MW00584443

ACQUIRING
THE MIND OF CHRIST

Embracing the Vision of the Orthodox Church

ACQUIRING
THE MIND OF CHRIST

Embracing the Vision of the Orthodox Church

Archimandrite Sergius (Bowyer)

MMXV

Acquiring the Mind of Christ:
Embracing the Vision of the Orthodox Church
© 2015, by Archimandrite Sergius Bowyer. All rights reserved.
General editor: Sergei Arhipov
Editor-in-chief: Priest Matthew Markewich
No portions of this book may be reproduced without the permission of the author.

Published by:
St. Tikhon's Monastery Press
175 St. Tikhon's Road
Waymart, Pennsylvania 18472
Printed in the United States of America

ISBN: 978-0-9905029-9-9

"AND LET THIS mind be in you which is also in Christ Jesus…"

-Philippians 2:5

THE GOSPEL PRECEPTS contain God's revelation of Himself. The more deeply we enter into their spirit, the more specific will be our vision of God. And when these commandments, by His good providence, come to be the one and only principle of our whole being, both temporal and eternal, then we too, 'shall be like Him; for we shall see Him as He is' (1 John 3:2).

-Archimandrite Sophrony, *We Shall See Him As He Is* (Essex: St. John the Baptist Monastery, 2004), 149.

Special thanks to:

St. Tikhon's Monastery Community
St. Tikhon's Seminary Community
Dr. Harry Boosalis
Priest Matthew Markewich
Matushka Rebekah Markewich
Rdr. John Kennerk

Contents

FOREWORD

OUR LORD AND GOD and Savior Jesus Christ is the proto-archetypal man. He reveals to us not only perfect God, but also perfect man, as man is intended to be, showing us the potential of everyone born into this world. This potential is to have the "fullness of the Godhead dwelling in us" (Col. 2:9), not by nature, but by Grace, so "that we might become partakers of the Divine Nature" (II Pet. 1:4) and become "temples of the Holy Spirit" (I Cor. 6:19). To deny the Lord Jesus Christ is to deny our true selves, "hid with Christ in God" (Col. 3:3). The purpose for which we were created is that we might know God and through this knowledge (which denotes communion) become eternal, sharing in God's very life.[1]

Our task is great: to acquire Christ, to put on Christ, and to acquire the Mind of Christ. How are we to begin? The Church's Mind is the Mind of Christ. The way the Church thinks is the way we need to learn to think about God, ourselves, each other, and the world. If we fail to understand that our thinking has a tremendous impact on how we live

---

[1] See John 17:3.

and act, then we have already missed the mark. As one modern Elder said, "our thoughts determine our lives."[2]

We must examine ourselves and realize the tremendous impact the modern non-Christian worldview has on us as Orthodox Christians. We must seek to put on the new man and to put off the old with his thinking, habits, and perspectives. Only the radical change afforded to us by profound repentance has the potential to remake us in the likeness of Christ.

I offer the thoughts contained in this book not as an end, but as a beginning, looking to challenge modern thinking and presuppositions that are commonly held by all of us, but not often perceived or understood. The contents of this book are meant to be a compass to point in a more Orthodox direction. It is important to remember that what we believe will have a direct impact on how we act inside and outside the Church, and ultimately what we perceive the mission of the Orthodox Church to be. It is our task then to leave aside those things which are not conducive to our salvation—especially opinions, thoughts, or mindsets—that will not help us attain our ultimate goal: communion with God.

The task of repentance is literally a change of mind. Our goal is to acquire the Mind of Christ which is the Mind of the Church. The Scriptures show us this Mind. The Church services reveal to us this Mind. The Fathers and saints of the Church open us to this Mind. We must divest ourselves of the old to reinvest with the new. Let each of us begin anew this day seeking that which is above, forgetting what

---

[2] Elder Thaddeus of Vitovnica.

is behind, and pressing onward to the high calling in Christ Jesus our Lord.

Archimandrite Sergius
Feast of the Holy Apostle Mark
April 25, 2015

LITURGY AS LIFE

[Elder] Sophrony said many times that the conditions of the modern world are such that hesychastic life, as he himself had known it in the desert, is no longer possible. But the only thing which is left to us now is the Liturgy. If we celebrate the Liturgy with reverence and attention, we find as much grace and even more than can be found in the hesychastic life. For this reason, if we keep the Liturgy properly, there is hope for a renewal, maybe even for a renaissance of the whole world. This general crisis that we face nowadays—and it may intensify—will force many people to look for a spiritual solution and may lead them back to the Church. And if this is already happening with a small number of people, God is able to generalize it. He was very optimistic— *"As long as we keep the Liturgy,"* he used to say.[1]

[1] Archimandrite Zacharias (Zachariou), *Remember Thy First Love* (Dalton: Mount Thabor Publishing, 2010), 396.

THE LITURGY IS THE HEART of the Orthodox Christian experience, the place where one meets the Lord and learns to abide and live with Him. Not only this; it is through the Liturgy that one finds and works out one's salvation. In the liturgical life of the Orthodox Church, we find the Mind of the Church, which is the Mind of Christ. Through regular participation in the cycle of services throughout the year, and the Holy Mysteries, we absorb and acquire this Mind and make it our own, enabling us to learn how not only to think, but also how to understand the world, God, ourselves, and each other. We must never see the Liturgy and the liturgical life of the Church as something extra. It is through the grace that we receive at each Liturgy that we are enabled to enter eternity, and are empowered to escape corruption, sin, and death, because what we are offered and receive is nothing other than the Life of God Himself.

In our modern American society, many things about the way we live and how we learn are antithetical to Orthodox Christian spirituality. What is it that epitomizes the world if not the frenzy and busyness of day-to-day life? Counter to this, what is it that characterizes Orthodox spiritual ethos and experience if not *hesychia*[2] or stillness? Indeed, the root of healing, of freedom from the passions, and the beginning of the knowledge of God is to be found in the Psalmist's words: "Be still and know that I am God" (Ps. 45:11 LXX). It is hesychia which leads us to the knowledge of God, and concurrently to a knowledge of ourselves; it provides the remedy for

---

[2] *Hesychia,* meaning an inner stillness of thoughts related to the practice of pure prayer of the heart.

the insanity of our modern world. The Church provides the oasis in the liturgical life for her members to be still and know.

Hesychia does not imply an absence or an emptiness. It is to be present with all of our heart, standing before the mystery of ourselves and God with one thought: the Lord our God.[3] Prayer as listening is our first step towards hearing God. Hesychia does not mean by definition that we are silent, but rather watchful, waiting for God expectantly with faith. Indeed, the twofold movement shown to us by the Prodigal Son in the Gospel of St. Luke reveals the content of real prayer and spiritual life: we must first come back to ourselves before we can return to our Father. Without a return to ourselves, we have no basis on which to open a dialogue with God, for we will be speaking outside of our heart, outside of ourselves. The Fathers say that if we wish to ascend to heaven, we must enter the heart, and there we will find the rungs of the ladder by which we will begin the ascent.

The Liturgy informs the heart and changes us imperceptibly. St. Maximus the Confessor tells us that just being present at the Liturgy ontologically alters us for the better, from a lower to a higher state.[4] St. John of Kronstadt even said, "If one was to put all of the world's most precious things on one side of a scale, and the Divine Liturgy on the other, the scales

---

[3] The Jesus Prayer is considered monologistic, or a prayer of one thought: "Lord Jesus Christ, Son of God, have mercy on me."

[4] "The invisibly present grace of the Holy Spirit" acts "during the Holy Synaxis" in an altogether special way, "changing and transforming and truly reshaping each into a more divine state" (St. Maximus the Confesser, *Mystagogy*, 24, quoted in Nikolaos Loudovikos, *A Eucharistic Ontology: Maximus the Confessor's Eschatological Ontology of Being as Dialogical Reciprocity*, trans. Elizabeth Theokritoff [Brookline: Holy Cross Orthodox Press, 2010], 15).

would tip completely in favor of the Divine Liturgy."[5] He qualified this statement by explaining that

> the Divine Liturgy is truly a heavenly service upon earth, during which God Himself, in a particular, immediate, and most close manner, is present and dwells with men, being Himself the invisible Celebrant of the service, offering and being offered. There is nothing upon earth holier, higher, grander, more solemn, more life-giving than the Liturgy.... When the Lord descended upon Mount Sinai the Hebrew people were ordered to previously prepare and cleanse themselves. In the Divine service we have not a lesser event than God's descent upon Mount Sinai, but a greater one: here before us is the very face of God the Lawgiver.[6]

It is through the Liturgy that we learn how to live a spiritual life, for it shows us a pattern of how to take this world and to offer it up in an *Anaphora*,[7] invoking the Holy Spirit on everyone, everything, and every situation. This in turn grants the possibility of everything in our personal world of becoming eucharistic, an encounter with God, a point of contact and not of separation. Our main task as liturgical beings is to take our

---

[5] Emmanuel Hatzidekis, *The Heavenly Banquet* (Clearwater: Orthodox Witness, 2013), 46.

[6] St. John of Kronstadt, *My Life in Christ,* trans. E.E. Goulaeff (Jordanville: Holy Trinity Monastery, 2000), 390.

[7] *Anaphora,* the section of the Divine Liturgy where the priest offers and consecrates the bread and wine to be the Body and Blood of Christ.

world and re-connect it to God in thanksgiving (i.e., to make it eucharistic).

The first-created man, by severing the tie of this world from God (when he began to use the world apart from God for its own sake), became the first official "consumer." We on the other hand must reverse the Fall in our own lives by re-connecting this world and our lives back to the source of all: Christ, the Life-giver and Creator. If the Liturgy of the Church can permeate every part of our life, we will no longer be consumers as Adam had become, but rather communicants as Adam once was, the world becoming a window and a mirror for us to see the invisible and almighty power of God.[8]

The saving works of the God-man Jesus Christ (e.g., the Incarnation, the Cross, the Tomb, the Resurrection, and the Ascension) have passed into, and are now manifested within, the sacramental life of the Church. According to St. Leo the Great, this sacramental liturgical worship is the primary revelation and entrance into these saving acts for the world.[9]

It is paramount that the utmost care be taken to preserve these precious and beautiful flowers that have budded forth from the Gospel of our Lord Jesus Christ and find their fullest manifestation within the cycle of services in the Church. It is imperative to understand that he who cares for the Liturgy and ministers unto the Lord takes care of the Lord Himself.

It must be stated and emphasized that Orthodox Christian life is, by definition, a liturgical life. To fail to recognize this is to fail to find the key to the mystery of Orthodox Christianity.

---

[8] See Rom. 1:20

[9] St. Leo the Great's homily, *On the Lord's Ascension* quoted in *Synaxarion of the Lenten Triodion and Pentecostarion* (Rives Junction: HDM, 1999), 219.

Professor Constantine Scouteris explains this unbreakable connection between salvation and worship:

> In the Tradition of the Eastern Orthodox Church, doctrine and worship are inseparable. Worship is, in a certain sense, doctrinal testimony, reference to the events of Revelation. Thus, "dogmas are not abstract ideas in and for themselves but revealed and saving truths and realities intended to bring mankind into communion with God." One could say without hesitation that, according to Orthodox understanding, the fullness of theological thought is found in the worship of the Church. This is why the term Orthodoxy is understood by many not as "right opinion," but as "right doxology," [that is,] "right worship."[10]

The Liturgy is meant to become our life, and the continual entry into the new life that is granted to us in Christ. The Church's teachings are inseparable from the Liturgy, and all of her theological definitions that she proclaims (such as the Creed) are confirmed by and revealed through the Liturgy. It is primarily through this liturgical life that we begin to enter the corporate dogmatic visionary consciousness of the Church. Fr. Georges Florovsky once explained that "the Church is first of all a worshiping community. Worship comes first and then doctrine and discipline."[11] The Church has not grown out of

---

[10] Constantine Scouteris, *Ecclesial Being: Contributions to Theological Dialogue* (South Canaan: Mount Thabor Publishing, 2005), 88.

[11] Hilarion Alfeyev, *The Mystery of Faith: An Introduction to the Teachings and the Spirituality of the Orthodox Church* (Crestwood: St. Vladimir's Seminary Press, 2011), 167.

dogmatic formulas, nor even Holy Scripture, but out of right worship, uniting us into one Spirit in the one Body of Christ.

We must always know and remember what it means to be Orthodox: our whole life is to become a Liturgy, an Anaphora; a constant offering up of our talents, our time, our hearts, and our world to Christ. Our life can become a prayer when we continually turn our hearts to Christ and His saints for help. For what is prayer if not the turning of the heart to dialogue with God rather than a circular monologuing with our ego and passions? In this way, we will not only go to the Liturgy once or twice a week in the Church building, but rather we bring the Liturgy into every part of our lives, calling down the Holy Spirit to sanctify our families, our workplaces, our cars, our homes, and even our enemies.

The Life of Christ that is given to us can only become ours when we, in imitation of the Lord, also offer up our life and our heart, that we might be able to receive Him. There must be an exchange of lives. When we receive the Eucharist, there must be a tremendous effort in our own life to become like unto Christ Himself, especially by being obedient to His words.

Without the willingness to offer ourselves on the altar of sacrifice, to carry our Cross, to forsake all that we have, it will be certain that we will not have room enough within ourselves to receive and contain His infinite and eternal Life. The mystery of the Cross working in our life, when we are personally affixed to it, is God stretching us, that we can contain more of His grace; that one day we might be able to contain not only Him but all of mankind in our heart.

Our task is to acquire the Mind of Christ, not by imitation, but through an impartation and participation. This only happens through the Church by grace, informing our heart so that we understand the world in and through Christ. The only way to acquire this is through living the Liturgy. Our personal interior prayer life must be strong and joined to dedicated regular attendance at all of the services. We will never have time for the Church and the things of God unless we make time, prioritizing our life so as to put God first. If we say that we love God, that means, says St. Silouan the Athonite, that we pray. There are two sides of the life of prayer which are inseparably bound: personal and corporate. We need both if we are to make progress, for they both nourish each other, strengthening and reinforcing each other respectively.

Today is the day of salvation and the time is far spent. It is time to awake from the slumber of the world and to put on Christ, beseeching Him to grant us a continual renewal of our repentance and of our life in the Church. It is time to put spiritual capital into our bank account in eternity, so that when we fail, we will be received into the eternal habitations. The Church's Liturgy and a life of personal prayer prepare us to live in God's presence, to endure God's presence, and to love God's presence. We must make this preparation in this world, otherwise, in the world to come, there will be no more time for us to make the appropriate adjustment to that which "eye hath not seen, nor ear heard, neither have entered into the heart of man" (1 Cor. 2:9).

We may not ever find the perfect prayer that a few in a generation will reach. However, the Liturgy is perfect hypostatic prayer. Elder Zacharias of Essex tells us that the energy of this prayer upholds the universe.[12] We need not despair of our lack of perfection in prayer, but rather hasten to enter into

---

[12] (Zachariou), *Remember Thy First Love,* 239.

the Church's perfect hypostatic prayer, which saves us and the world. Our work as Orthodox is liturgical: serving and living the Liturgy, and through this, bringing the world into the Church. We can never underestimate the power of the Liturgy and its ability to transform and inform the heart. Our primary tool for evangelism to those inside and outside the Church is serving the Liturgy and the services of the Church. It is this which constitutes the sanctification of the world and grants us an opportunity to participate in the holiness of God Himself.

Therefore, we must always remember that the Church and its Liturgy are the Kingdom, the world to come, present in our midst today. St. Nicholas Cabasilas says, "What is the kingdom if not this Holy Bread and this Holy Cup?"[13] We must beware of supposing that heaven is something that is only in the future. As Metropolitan Hierotheos Vlachos states:

> We Orthodox are not waiting for the end of history and the end of time, but through living in Christ we are running to meet the end of history and thus already living the life expected after the Second Coming.[14]

This is what the saints show us. This is what the monastics remind us. This is what we are called to. In the Church, the Kingdom is present and revealed, but yet to be consummated. This is the Church. This is the Liturgy. This is our new life in

---

[13] Hieromonk Gregorios, *The Divine Liturgy: A Commentary in the Light of the Fathers*, trans. Elizabeth Theokritoff (Columbia: Newrome Press, 2010), 298.

[14] Hierotheos Vlachos, *Orthodox Psychotherapy: The Science of the Fathers,* trans. Esther Williams (Levadia: Birth of the Theotokos Monastery, 2006), 25.

Christ which He calls us to: "Come, all things have been pre-pared...." Our task is to do what we can and leave the rest to God. Our part may be a small offering, but it might very well be the widow's two mites which purchase for us the Kingdom.

PRAYER AS COMMUNION

The basic condition for the Prayer of the Heart is the belief that it is not merely prayer but rather true communion with God.[1]

Without real prayer there is no real life, and when we touch true prayer, we find it to be one of the greatest miracles of all....

ACCORDING TO ST. JOHN CLIMACUS, prayer is defined as "converse and union with God."[2] It is this personal conversation with God that effects union with Him, enabling us to fulfill our task of actualizing our salvation. If prayer is right, the Fathers say, then everything else will be right. Our task in this short earthly life is to resume the dialogue that was lost with God in Paradise; to learn how to orient the heart, tuning its antennae to the frequency of God's life and grace. It is in this way we acquire eternal life and our salvation.

---

[1] Archimandrite Aimilianos, *The Church at Prayer* (Alhambra: Sebastian Press, 2012), 44.

[2] St. John Climacus, *The Ladder of Divine Ascent,* trans. Holy Transfiguration Monastery (Brookline: Holy Transfiguration Monastery, 2010), 212.

It is not the purpose of this short exhortation to explain all of the dynamics of inner prayer and the vicissitudes we will face. It is, however, our task to once again remind all that without prayer, whether personal or corporate, there is no salvation. It is imperative that all Christians everywhere, no matter their place or rank, must learn to pray with their heart, deeply committing to a life of prayer if they expect to know God and do His will.[3]

Prayer generates prayer. The Holy Scriptures tell us that "God grants prayer to the one who prays." Our task is to begin simply, entering into the dialogue with God and renouncing the monologue with our ego and passions.

If we wish to make progress in the area of prayer and be sensitized to spiritual things we must fulfill three basic tasks:

First, we must be deeply committed to a certain amount of prayer at a certain time every day, without fail. We must fulfill this task, not just as a rule or an obligation, but out of concern for cultivating our relationship with God. This is our salvation and joy. (Our time of prayer can be in the morning and/or evening as the circumstances of our life permit.)

Second, as St. Theophan the Recluse says, we must always pray as if we have never prayed before. This means we always approach the mystery of God without expectation or illusion, without letting our past success or failure distract us from our present contact with the Lord. As God can only be found in the present, nostalgia can be harmful to prayer. In addition, imagination[4] should never be used when praying as it can potentially be the conduit for demonic energy.

---

[3] See 1 John 2:17

[4] Imagination, often called "fantasy," defined as the part of us which

Third, we must always be willing to start again no matter how long it has been since we have prayed or what the outcome, good or bad, has been in the past. This also applies to our repentance so that no matter what we have done, seen, thought, or heard, we approach God for forgiveness, in search of our medicine. St. Paul reminds us: "Forgetting those things which are behind, and reaching forth unto those things which are before, I press toward the mark for the prize of the high calling of God in Christ Jesus" (Phil. 3:13-14), for "a broken and contrite heart, O God, Thou wilt not despise" (Ps. 50:19 LXX).

The Apostle exhorts all Christians to "pray without ceasing" (1 Thes. 5:17). This task is great and is often one of the most difficult to pursue, precisely because prayer affords such great reward: peace, life, renewal, enlightenment, joy in the Holy Spirit, and ultimately our salvation. Our Lord asks each one of us: "Could you not watch with me one hour?" (Matt. 26:40). "Watch and pray, that you enter not into temptation" (Matt. 26:41) and fall away from your spiritual life. "What I say to you, I say to all: Watch!" (Mark 13:37).

In this context of prayer, watchfulness is the key to our inner life. It allows for a healthy distance from our thoughts and potential release from our passions. The Jesus Prayer is essential in helping us to build up a sense of watchfulness in our heart and thoughts, enabling us to detach from them to some degree; for we are not our thoughts. St. Theophan tells us[5] that the principal asceticism of the spiritual life is keeping

---

produces mental images. While imagination is itself good, its use during prayer is considered dangerous by the Fathers. In prayer, it opens the door to demonic deception, and therefore spiritual delusion.

[5] *The Art of Prayer: An Orthodox Anthology,* ed. Igumen Chariton. trans.

our mind and heart from passionate movement and thought.[6] The Jesus Prayer, "Lord Jesus Christ, Son of God, have mercy on me," is an essential tool for enabling us to overcome the deadly sinful movements of the mind and heart. This short prayer is a remedy and defense against every kind of darkness. St. Isaac the Syrian even says that the Name of Christ *is* light. When we use this light against the onslaught of temptations, we dispel their darkness.

Elder Zacharias explains that the easiest way to become the Temple of the Holy Spirit is through the invocation of the Name of Jesus Christ. In this way, we open the heart to the grace of God. However, Elder Sophrony reminds us that it is essential to love the One we invoke. And how do we love Him? The Lord tells us, "If you love me, keep my commandments" (John 14:15). Since these commandments exceed human measure, they can only be fulfilled with the power of prayer.

If we are to start the task of prayer, we must begin immediately. We should not be motivated by a lot of excitement or self-praise, thinking that we are owed something great for our spiritual effort. It is our privilege and joy to converse with our God, being the purpose for which we were created.

It is imperative that we see personal and corporate prayer as two sides of the same coin. Corporate liturgical prayer life in the Church feeds into and provides invaluable and essential shape for our interior life. Corporate prayer life can become dead and frozen without the inner attention and fire which personal prayer gives us. Inner life, if not well-grounded in the liturgical life of the Church, can possibly lead us to delusion.

E. Kadloubovsky and E. M. Palmer (London: Faber & Faber, 1997), 24.

    [6] See Matt. 5:27-29.

Today is the day of salvation, and we must never put off prayer for another time. Every moment is the moment to turn to the Lord, to thank the Lord for all His innumerable benefits, to beseech aid from on high, to repent and ask for forgiveness, and to ask His blessing. The most essential part of prayer is the inner turning of the heart to the Lord.

The classic textbook definition of prayer given by St. Theophan the Recluse is "standing with the mind in the heart before the Lord."[7] It is imperative that, as we pray, our attention (our *nous*)[8] remains in our heart[9] as much as possible. As the nous wanders, we simply bring it back to the heart and to the words of the prayer.

Another essential key to this new life of prayer is learning to listen to God. God is always speaking to us but we are often so busy monologuing with ourselves that we may not be able to hear Him. It is important that we not only approach prayer as union with God but also with a receptive listening heart, waiting on the Lord like the Prophet Samuel: "Yes, Lord, thy servant is listening" (1 King. 3:10 LXX). This means that we cultivate silence (hesychia or stillness) and watchfulness in our prayer time so that it is not just filled with our requests; we make room to hear from the Lord His requests from us. However, He won't always speak to us in the manner in which we might expect. Sometimes it may be a verse from Scripture,

---

[7] Chariton, *The Art of Prayer,* 70.

[8] *Nous,* defined as the "eye of the heart." The nous is the center of the attention, the part of the soul which actively perceives the inner and spiritual world; it beholds rather than considers. It must not be confused with reason or logic. Nous is often translated as intellect or mind.

[9] Heart, defined as the physical organ, but also the center of the soul's powers.

a verse from the Fathers, a sense in our own heart of intuition or conscience, or just the peace of God. We must be open and ready for any way God chooses to reveal Himself, always willing to confirm the word with those who have a good witness in the Church (e.g., our priest, spiritual father, knowledgeable trusted layman; the point is to have a good reference outside ourselves). Monologistic prayer, or literally 'the prayer of one thought' (the Jesus Prayer), helps us learn how to speak with and listen to God.

This book includes a short prayer rule that can help us to make a beginning.[10] It takes approximately ten minutes, the minimum time for the heart to reorient itself to a better spiritual state. It is by no means a static rule, and we must continue to "press into the kingdom" more wholeheartedly each day. As we press into prayer in the long term, we need to extend our time with the Lord in an incremental way until we have the right amount of helpful spiritual tension.[11]

Here is the basic rule:

Trisagion
Psalm 50
The Creed
Five prostrations (*using Jesus Prayer*)
Five minutes of the Jesus Prayer

---

[10] See page 157.

[11] Ideally, laymen should try to slowly work up to praying 20 to 30 minutes a day, priests at least one hour, and monastics more than one hour. This is just a general rule of thumb. What is most important is that we do something every day. We should never lessen our ideal even when circumstances do not permit us to fulfill our good intentions.

Any appropriate prayers (e.g., morning or evening,
akathists, etc.)
A chapter from the Gospels
"It is truly meet…"
Normal ending: "Through the prayers…"

This rule can be expanded: e.g., 50 prostrations and 50 minutes saying the Jesus Prayer, or small sections of other spiritual reading to be read after the Gospel, etc. The entire cycle can even be repeated again if desired. However, what is most important is that we understand from the beginning that prayer is a matter of constancy and consistency, incrementally building our time with the Lord in a measured and regulated way. We do not want to pray merely so as to fulfill some sense of religious obligation. We do not want to pray so that we feel better about ourselves. God forbid! We want a living, life-giving relationship with our Creator and Lord Jesus Christ, to be sensitized to His voice and to true spiritual reality. This can only be achieved by humble, committed, and patient prayer. We must always remember that it is the content of the humble and contrite prayer of the publican that justifies us: "God be merciful to me a sinner" (Luke 18:13). Prayer is not just a matter of the actual words said, but more so of the right and contrite disposition of the heart when speaking with God.

St. Theoleptos of Philadelphia reminds us that we must never neglect prostrations.[12] The body must be included in this dialogue with the Lord. Our prayer needs to come from our heart, both the spiritual and the bodily. Through prayer,

---

[12] For example, see *On Inner Work in Christ,* in *The Philokalia: The Complete Text,* vol. 4, trans. and ed. G.E.H. Palmer, Philip Sherrard, Kallistos Ware (London: Faber & Faber, 1999), 185.

we journey deeper into the body, concerned with its transfiguration, rather than escaping from it. The body is meant to
become the Temple of the Holy Spirit.[13] It is through profound
prayer of tearful contrition to the Lord that both the soul
and the body are sanctified. Therefore we must never neglect
prostrations as they help to bring the mind and body together
before the Lord, creating a prayerful dialogue from our whole
person.

In addition, reading the Gospel and spiritual reading is
necessary during prayer. It is during this time that the heart
can become still, lucid, and open to the grace and life which
are hidden within the words themselves. Christ tells us that
the words He gives to us "are spirit, and they are life" (John
6:63). If we are open and receptive, the Spirit of the Gospel
can enter into us, profoundly altering our heart, sanctifying
us. Further, not only will we change; through this prayerful
encounter we have frequent opportunity for God to speak
directly to us in a profound and real way.

This chapter's exhortation to prayer is not a definitive guide
but rather a beginning for us who have not yet endeavored
to begin this blessed and life-giving work. Prayer is the only
bridge over the despondency of the world with its death, sins,
and passions. It gives light to the mind, helping us to slowly
see ourselves as we are, and God as He is. It enables us to overcome temptation and weaknesses. It has the potential to heal
our spiritual infirmities. Persistent and patient prayer is the
answer to almost all the questions we have; this is so because
it grants us God's grace and peace. It also brings us to a saving

---

[13] This is why the Orthodox Church does not practice cremation.

knowledge of the true God, going above and beyond rational thought.

It cannot be stated enough that it is essential to begin again today. Prayer generates prayer. The Fathers tell us that prayer will teach us and be our guide if we are devoted to it.[14] It is the quintessential practice for all Christians. If we say we love God, we pray; if we say that we love each other, we pray for each other. Our life of prayer fulfills the commandment on which hang all the Law and the Prophets: to love God and to love our neighbor. Prayer is simple, but it can be arduous. Prayer is fought against on all sides. It can be our guide and light in all things. Prayer in its highest form, St. Gregory of Sinai says, is God Himself. Let us begin again our conversation with God this very moment, thereby moving forward to our union and salvation in Christ our God.

---

[14] Prayer does not, however, take the place of necessary spiritual direction and confession. Rather, it will lead us to them.

THE ANGRY GOD OF ANSELM

ANSELM OF CANTERBURY'S doctrine of the Atonement[1] has been said by some to be a key to understanding the rejection of the saving truth of Christianity by an untold number of people in the last millennium. They reject Anselm's portrait of an angry God who is in need of being appeased; who pronounces people guilty or not. The modern Anselmian doctrine of Atonement reduces the powerfully transformative aspect of the Gospel to a juridical concept, drained of its life. The purpose of this chapter will be to briefly reveal and discuss some of the underpinnings of the Anselmian doctrine of Atonement: why they are harmful to the New Life in Christ, and by contrast, to show that the fullness of the Gospel message is found in the biblical-patristic context of the Orthodox Church. This is not a needless inquiry, but rather one which is necessary if we desire salvation.

One of the greatest miracles for people of ancient times was coming to know of the Gospel message: that the True and Living God was Love; a personal and living God Who gave

---

[1] Atonement, defined as man's restoration to a right relationship with God.

His only Begotten Son, "not to condemn the world but that the world through Him might be saved" (John 3:17). Gods of ancient times were remote (e.g., the Greek god Zeus), murderous (the Hindu goddess of death, Kali), and even required sacrifices such as children (the Ammonite tribal god, Moloch, cf. Lev. 20:2). The concept alone that the Christian God was a personal God of mercy, love, and forgiveness, powerfully attracted great numbers; many even willingly faced the possibility of martyrdom for confessing their faith.[2]

Christ came to bring Life to us who were dead in Adam[3] because He Himself is "the Way, the Truth and the Life" (John 14:6). This is the foundation which the first Christians, from St. Paul the Apostle onward, understood as the key to salvation: that "forasmuch then as the children are partakers of flesh and blood, He likewise took part of the same; that through death He might destroy him who had the power of death, that is the devil … abolish[ing] death and [bringing] life and immortality to light" through the Gospel (Heb. 2:14; II Tim. 1:10).[4]

For the first thousand years of Christianity, the Gospel message was not understood from the now common Scholastic mindset of Anselm. Today, Anselm's ideas are unfortunately the most dominant perspective of Christianity in the Western world, both Protestant and Roman Catholic. The

---

[2] Christianity is the only religion which guarantees reconciliation with God and forgiveness of sins. "For if we confess our sins, He is faithful and just and will forgive us and cleanse us from all unrighteousness … For God was in Christ reconciling the world unto Himself" (I John 1:9, II Cor. 5:19).

[3] See I Cor. 15:22.

[4] The paschal troparion, being one of the earliest troparia of the 2nd and 3rd centuries, explains that it was not possible for the Life of all, Jesus Christ, to see corruption, but that rather He "is Risen … trampling down death by death and upon those in the tombs bestowing Life."

early Christians, just as today's Orthodox Christians, under-stood that Christ releases us from sin by destroying its root, death. Those who have put on Christ are no longer slaves of sin, "because you are not under the Law but under grace" (Rom. 6:14). For the "Law of the Spirit of Life in Christ Jesus has set you free from the Law of sin and death" (Rom. 8:2).

Anselm, the Roman Catholic Archbishop of Canterbury in the 11th century (1033-1109), was the father of modern Scho-lastic theology and philosophy. He has been seen by some to be the first to develop a doctrine of Atonement apart from the Church's biblical-patristic heritage. By adjusting his theology to fit his society's understanding of the time, Anselm utilizes a feudal ethic[5] to rationally discern the unfathomable depth of the mystery of God.

Anselm can be seen as a bridge between St. Augustine of Hippo and Thomas Aquinas. By using classical philosophy and logic as instruments of discovery (instead of a means of interpretation), Anselm's doctrines made the infinite truth of God subject to a created finite intellect. In contrast, the Scrip-tures are quite clear that God's revelation "is not after man. For I neither received it of man, neither was I taught it, but by the revelation of Jesus Christ" (Gal. 1:11-12).[6]

The current Roman Catholic position, originating from Anselm, officially states that "justification has been merited for us by the Passion of Christ, who offered himself on the cross as a living victim … whose blood has become the instrument

---

[5] In feudal cultures, a servant owed a debt of fealty (obedience) to a lord in exchange for protection and livelihood. Anselm uses this model in his theology of the Atonement.

[6] See also Is. 55:8.

of atonement for the sins of all men."[7] The question then is raised: How does this Atonement happen and who is it offered to? The Orthodox likewise see Christ as the One Who gave His life as a ransom for many.[8]

Christ is the ransom that was paid to death as St. Athanasius the Great (4th century) says in light of Hosea 13:14: "The ransom was offered to death on behalf of all so that by it He once more opened the way to the heavens."[9] In stark contrast, the Anselmian Roman Catholic doctrine asserts that the debt was paid to God the Father to satisfy His infinite wrath, a byproduct of offense to His justice and honor. This doctrine of Atonement also states that sin is an affront to the Divinity, for which mere man cannot make reparation; it regards sin as a transgression in the legal sense rather than the Orthodox perspective of an illness of the heart and will. In this light, Anselm's assumption is that a "divine honor" has been wounded and is in need of "satisfaction."[10] This necessitates a legal transaction by which Christ pays the Father with His own blood the debt incurred by man's sin. The Resurrection of Christ does not occupy a central place in man's redemption.[11]

---

[7] Geoffrey Chapman, *Catechism of the Catholic Church* (London: Burns and Oates, 2006), 433.

[8] See Mark 10:45.

[9] St. Athanasius, *On the Incarnation,* 25 *PG* 25 140C quoted in Michael Azkoul, *Once Delivered to the Saints* (Seattle: Saint Nectarios Press, 2000), 128.

[10] Anselm of Canterbury, "Why God Became Man," in *Major Works,* 2.6, 1.8, 1.9., ed. Brian Davies and G. R. Evans (Oxford: Oxford University Press, 2008).

[11] Fixating on the Atonement, a modern Catholic theologian epitomizes this failure when he says that "the Resurrection of Christ was not strictly speaking, the chief, or even a contributing cause to our redemption.... The Catholic Church regards the Resurrection as an integral, though not

If God then is infinitely offended by our sin and is therefore in need of some infinite "satisfaction," many can rightly (and unfortunately) begin to equate this God with a sadistic image of a father compelled by honor to inflict punishment. Thus God is made subject to justice. By subjecting God to this law of necessity and ascribing to Him human characteristics such as vengeance and anger, we make it appear that it is God who is in need of healing, and not man.

However, God never changes, for it is not God that is at enmity with man, but man who is at enmity with God.[12] The foundation of a proper understanding of salvation is that God does not change: "Jesus Christ is the same yesterday, today and forever" (Heb. 13:8). Thus, the Orthodox approach seeks to heal man, and not God, recognizing sin as a refusal of the Love of God, the entrance of death, and the deconstruction of the soul.

The Orthodox see the Fall of man from a medical perspective: as an illness of the heart that brings death by cutting off communion with the One Who is Life. Holistic healing is thus sought by the Orthodox with the end of restoring communion with God. The believer conquers death through participation in God's Life through the sacraments and ascetical discipline. Conversely, the Anselmian understanding essentially declares man "not guilty," and leaves him, unfortunately, unhealed and unchanged. This distorts the real message of Christian salvation: to "be partakers of the divine nature" (II Pet. 1:4).

---

an essential, element of Atonement" (Joseph Pohle, *Soteriology* [London: Herder, 1946], 102).

[12] See Hierotheos Vlachos, *The Mind of the Orthodox Church,* trans. Esther Williams (Levadia: Birth of the Theotokos Monastery, 1998), 170.

The formation of the Anselmian doctrine of Atonement is seen by modern commentators as "a revolution in theology,"[13] beginning "a new epoch in the theology of Atonement."[14] This new doctrine stemmed from several factors. Foremost, a characteristic influence of the legalistic Roman mindset is exhibited in Western theologians as early as Tertullian which encourages and supports a juridical conceptualization concerning the truths of the faith. Anselm drew from Tertullian who sees man's sin as a disturbance in the "divine order of justice,"[15] and makes penance a "satisfaction to the Lord."[16]

Another strong influence on Anselm was St. Augustine. Not only did Anselm utilize St. Augustine's concept of "limited Atonement,"[17] but he also used his methods of theological and philosophical experimentation. After Anselm's and subsequently Peter Abelard's "revolution" in Atonement theology, most in the West became further estranged from the Orthodox experience. Thus arose a host of new supposed "developments" in theology from Catholic and Protestant scholars: vicarious

---

[13] Harold Berman, *Law and Revolution: The Formation of the Western Legal Tradition* (Cambridge: Harvard University Press, 1983), 175; see also Azkoul, *Once Delivered to the Saints,* 131.

[14] See *The Catholic Encyclopedia,* Vol. 2, ed. Charles Herberman (New York: The Gilmary Society), 56.

[15] It must be remembered that Tertullian was a lawyer.

[16] Anselm, *Basic Writings,* in "On Repentance," Ch. 5.9. trans. S.N. Deane (LaSalle: Open Court, 1962).

[17] Limited Atonement, meaning that the salvific effects of Christ's atoning sacrifice do not extend to all mankind. St. Augustine said that through the Fall of Adam, "the whole mass of the human race is condemned, for he [Adam] who at first gave entrance to sin has been punished with all his posterity ... but many more are left under punishment than are delivered from it, in order that it may thus be shown what was due to all" (*The City of God,* XXI, 12 MD; quoted in Azkoul, *Once Delivered to the Saints,* 132n).

Atonement, which placates God's anger;[18] Don Scotus' "merits" for the predestined; and indulgences, which apparently can "pay" the Church the fee for the offenders' sins.

Four hundred years after Anselm, the Roman Catholic Council of Trent, in response to the Protestant Reformation, was compelled to define the exact nature of Atonement in agreement with Anselm's new understanding. This Council established that at the core of Anselmian Atonement was St. Augustine's doctrine of Original Sin.[19]

The Augustinian doctrine of Original Sin, which entails all of Adam's posterity inheriting guilt, sets certain parameters for the Anselmian doctrine that do not exist in the Ortho-dox biblical-patristic mindset. Due to a faulty translation of Romans 5:12 in St. Jerome's Vulgate, St. Augustine formulates the doctrine that not only do all men inherit mortality and the inclination to sin, but they are guilty and legally liable before God for Adam's sin. This doctrine profoundly affects the perspective of *how* one is saved and *from what* he is saved. St. Augustine makes a twofold distinction: a hereditary moral disability (the inclination to sin) and an inherited legal

---

[18] "Christ endured for us those sufferings which we deserved to suffer in consequence of the sin of our first parents..." (Thomas Aquinas, *Compendium of Theology,* Chapter 228, trans. Richard Regan [Oxford: Oxford University Press, 2009]).

[19] "In its second session, the Council of Trent was compelled to define the nature of Original Sin as the indispensable preliminary to the defini-tion of justification, because the whole doctrine of justification is dependent upon the definition of Original Sin" (David Weaver, "The Exegesis of Ro-mans 5:12 Among the Greek Fathers and Its Implication for the Doctrine of Original Sin: The 5th-12th Centuries, Part II," *St. Vladimir's Theological Quarterly,* Vol. 29, No. 2. [Crestwood: St. Vladimir's Seminary Press, 1985], 206).

liability (guilty before God for Adam's sin).[20] The Council proceeded to anathematize all who refused to accept the doctrine of Original Sin: i.e., that all had received Adam's guilt for his personal sin.[21]

In this system, if Christ paid the debt to the Father, and if the sacramental life placates the wrath of the Father, then isn't it no surprise that Protestantism developed as it did, questioning the need for the Church? It might be said that Anselm's doctrine makes the Protestant Reformation possible, even inevitable. Consequently we must ask: How then does Christ's saving act become effective for each person? And how is one freed from the Augustinian notion of Original Sin? For the Reformers, it was justification by faith alone, *sola fide,* which trusted in Christ's vicarious sacrifice[22] apart from the Church.

For Roman Catholics, justification came through the Pope and the Church by the grace of holy baptism.[23] Atonement theology effectively makes the Roman Catholic Church the means of a legal justification which pronounces 'not guilty' through the sacraments, rather than a process which restores the innate 'goodness' of man.

---

[20] See St. Augustine's *Unfinished Work against Julian* 3:24; *On the Nature of the Catholic Church* 1:40.

[21] *Decrees of the Ecumenical Councils,* from Council of Trent, Session 5:2-5, ed. Norman P. Tanner (London: Sheed and Ward, 1990), 666.

[22] Vicarious sacrifice is the belief that Christ receives the wrath and punishment of God the Father in our stead.

[23] Christ "merited justification for us by his most holy passion on the wood of the Cross, and made satisfaction to God the Father on our behalf; the instrumental cause is the sacrament of baptism, which is the sacrament of faith" (*Decrees of the Ecumenical Councils.* Council of Trent, Session 6, 673).

The loss of the patristic perspective meant the loss of the full experience of the Church. Without it, Roman Catholic theology often became a narrow juridical procedure overly focused on appeasing God's justice. This truncating of salvation is further reinforced by St. Augustine's non-Orthodox conception of grace. For St. Augustine, it seems that man may never participate in God's deifying energies, and therefore man and God remain forever external to each other. Ultimately, this leads to salvation not defined by communion with God, but rather primarily a moral and legal relationship.

In contrast, the Orthodox view of justification is being empowered by grace to live according to God's will. By living according to God's will, we effect our sanctification, thereby participating in God's life. By being united with the One Who overcomes death, we overcome sin and death, participating in His victory, making it our own. In the Orthodox perspective, Anselm's understanding of God's wrath and punishment are non-existent.

The Orthodox Church teaches that Christ, by His very Incarnation, takes away the sin of the world. St. Gregory the Theologian says the passage "the Word was made flesh" (John 1:14) is

> equivalent to that in which it is said that "He was made sin or a curse for us" (1 Cor. 5:21); not that the Lord was transformed into either of these—how could he be? But because by taking them upon him he took away our sins and bore our iniquities.[24]

---

[24] *Ancient Christian Commentary on Scripture: New Testament VII: First and Second Corinthians,* ed. Thomas C. Oden (New York: Routledge, 1999),

The beginning of the Orthodox view of the Atonement is the Incarnation. The middle of this process is the Cross, through which Christ, as St. Basil the Great explains, "gave Himself as a ransom to death, in which we were held captive, sold under sin, [and] descending through the Cross into hell—that He might fill all things with Himself—He loosed the pangs of death." The end of this process was His rising on the third day. Through His rising, He "made for all flesh a path to the Resurrection from the dead, since it was not possible for the Author of Life to be a victim of corruption."[25]

The heart of the matter of Orthodox redemption is *theosis*[26] and re-creation: "that in the dispensation of the fullness of time, He might gather together in one all things in Christ, both that which are in heaven and which are on the earth, even in Him" (Eph. 1:10). The Good News is that all of God's good creation[27] is called to enter the Church, which is union with the Triune God. Through the union of the natures in the God-man, our Lord Jesus Christ, the created world and the uncreated God are united.

In conclusion, our goal is not sin-redemption (i.e., Anselmian Atonement), but deification: that Christ might become formed in us. Through participating in Christ's Death and Resurrection in the sacramental-ascetical life, we become living members of Christ's Body in this world, delivered from death, the inclination to sin, and the darkness which comes from it. Being healed in our will by following the commandments of

---

253.

[25] The Anaphora of the Divine Liturgy of St. Basil the Great.

[26] *Theosis* is the process of participating in God's divine life. See 11 Pet. 1:4.

[27] See Gen. 1.

the Lord through the empowering action of the Holy Spirit, the Orthodox Christian is crucified with Christ, dying to the passions and sinful pleasures of the world (the old man), and becomes a partaker of the immortal energies of God through the Church. As Christ is continually formed in us,[28] we become by grace everything that God is by nature. This is the Orthodox view of the Atonement; this is the Orthodox view of salvation.

[28] See Gal. 4:19.

SEEDS OF HEAVEN AND HELL: PASSIONS, VIRTUES, AND LIFE AFTER DEATH

T HE SCRIPTURES and the patristic tradition of the Orthodox Church speak of only two realities after this world:
heaven and hell. These two words carry such heavy prejudice
and cause such intellectual bias in the modern world that their
reality is often totally obscured by preconceptions, making the
world inattentive and unable to hear the truth. And yet when
has the world ever been receptive to the truth? Popular opinion today often states that all religions have the same God, that
they all lead to the same place. And yet to become forgetful
of the judgment of God is to trivialize His existence, suggest-
ing that beyond this world there is no accountability; that the
righteous will stand with the unrepentant enjoying the same
place of Paradise. How could anyone think this could be so?

The Scriptures describe hell as an eternal destruction
and exclusion from the presence of the Lord (II Thes. 1:9); a
great tribulation (Rev. 2:22); a storing up of the wrath of God
(Rom. 2:5); a fury of fire which will consume the adversaries
of God (Heb. 10:27); the lake that burns with fire and sulfur

(Rev. 21:8); the nether gloom of darkness, reserved forever (II Pet. 2:17; Jude 13); a death, and the second death (Rom. 6:21; Rev. 2:11, 20:6-14, 21:8); a place where the worm does not die and the fire is never quenched (Mark 9:42-48; Is. 66:24); and a burning of unquenchable fire (Matt. 3:12).

From the biblical perspective, it is not God Who punishes man, but man who reaps what he has sown. The Apostle Paul tells us that

> [God] will render to every man according to his deeds: To them who by patient continuance in doing well seek for glory and honor and immortality, eternal life: But unto them that are contentious: ... indignation and wrath, tribulation and anguish, upon every soul of man that does evil, of the Jew first, and also of the Gentile; but glory, honor, and peace, to every man that works good, to the Jew first, and also to the Gentile (Rom. 2:6-10).

In the patristic understanding of the Orthodox Church, God's grace is one and the same, for God does not change. Yet how man relates to the uncreated grace of God in this world is the determining factor of his state in the afterlife. In the Gospel account of the rich man and Lazarus, we recall that the rich man was separated from Abraham's bosom "by a great chasm" that could not be spanned (Luke 16:26). Interestingly, Abraham still spoke with the rich man. Hell then cannot be seen as a place as we understand it, for St. John Chrysostom tells us that it is outside the created world.[1] Concerning this

---

[1] St. John Chrysostom, *Homily on Romans*, 31, quoted in Nikolaos

issue, St. John says we do not need to know where it is as we will not understand anyway. Rather our concern should be how to avoid it.[2]

The Eastern patristic consensus generally has a different focus from that of even the pre-schism Western Orthodox saints. Although both use the imagery of hell in the familiar fire-and-brimstone accounts, the Eastern focus tends to be more concerned with how heaven and hell are experienced in the heart of man through the virtues and the passions. St. Isaac the Syrian explains that Paradise is the love of God; the uncreated energy of God.[3] Yet, at the same time, this love is experienced as a scourge by unrepentant souls who cannot bear the pure glory of God. From the patristic perspective, God Himself is heaven for the saints and hell for the sinners.

We recall in the third chapter of the Book of Daniel the account of the three children in the fiery furnace. They serve as a type for this understanding of the afterlife. The three children who kept the commandments of God were not burnt by the fire but danced in the flames with the Angel of God, while those who heated the furnace out of malice and in wickedness were consumed by that very same fire.

Thus eternal life is light to those who have followed the commandments of the Lord and purified their heart and nous, whereas this same light will be darkness and misery to those who are living in a state contrary to the will of God. St. Maximus the Confessor explains that "the inheritance of the saints is God Himself, [and] he who is found worthy of this grace

Vassiliadis, *The Mystery of Death,* trans. Peter Chamberas (Athens: The Orthodox Brotherhood of Theologians, 1993), 520.

  [2] Ibid., 520.

  [3] *Ascetical Homilies,* 46.

will be beyond all ages, times, and places: he will have God Himself as his place."[4] In this life we are free, but after death, the potential tragedy that exists with human freedom will be honored: our choice is set.

St. John Chrysostom explains that there is a universal rule that we can use to discern the reality of heaven and hell: no one from among those who strive to please God and live a virtuous life according to the commandments will ever doubt the teaching about the judgment and hell.[5] From their own experience, they come to know and understand, to varying degrees, the death that sin causes and the life that virtue brings. St. Gregory of Sinai tells us that "passion-embroiled states are foretastes of hell's torments, just as the activity of the virtues is a foretaste of the kingdom of heaven."[6]

In our life, we place the different 'ingredients' within our souls, either the virtues or passions and sins. Once we encounter the uncreated flame of God's presence outside this world, these ingredients are indelibly 'baked' into our souls. For St. Gregory of Sinai, after death,

> [the] fire, darkness, the worm, and the nether world correspond to ubiquitous self-indulgence, total ignorance, all-pervasive lecherous pleasures, and the fearfulness and foul stench of sin [which already now] can be seen to be active, as

---

[4] St. Maximus the Confessor, *First Century on Theology,* 68, quoted in *Philokalia*, vol. 2, 128.

[5] *Homilies on Colossians,* 2. See Vassiliadis, *The Mystery of Death*, 508.

[6] *On Commandments and Doctrines,* 35, quoted in *Philokalia*, vol. 4, 218-9.

> foretastes and first fruits of hell's torments in sin-
> ners in whose souls they have taken root.[7]

Therefore, forgetfulness and doubt of hell stem from forgetfulness of God. Consequently, remembrance of God and the reality of hell is a property of saints, who forever consider themselves worthy of its flames. Metropolitan Hierotheos Vlachos
states,

> Contemporary men who see God on their ascetic
> pilgrimage affirm that as far as one repents and in
> *grace* experiences Hell, to that extent also grace,
> even without one's expecting it, is turned into
> uncreated light.[8]

The uncreated grace of God is one and the same "super-celestial
fire" which, according to St. John Climacus, burns some,
because they lack purification, while others it enlightens in
proportion to the progress they have made in virtue.[9]

The remembrance of hell is highly beneficial for the Christian, and it is recommended by many ascetic writers of the
Church as a restraint and cure against every evil. Just to consider the infinite, unchangeable loss of eternal peace, love,
and blessedness is enough to bring sobriety to the mind and
vigilance to the heart. The well-known expression given by St.
Silouan the Athonite, "Keep thy mind in hell and despair not,"
manifests the relevance and value of this remembrance.

---

[7] *On Commandments and Doctrines,* 34, quoted from *Philokalia,* vol. 4,
218.

[8] Hierotheos Vlachos, *Life After Death,* trans. Esther Williams (Levadia:
Birth of the Theotokos Monastery, 1996), 261.

[9] St. John Climacus, *Ladder of Divine Ascent,* 219.

Scripture tells us that heaven is the city of the Living God (Heb. 12:22); the assembly of the firstborn (Heb. 12:23); the inheritance which is imperishable, undefiled, and unfading (1 Pet. 1:4); a great banquet (Luke 14:15-24); a city of pure gold, like unto clear glass (Rev. 21:18); a place where the Lord God Almighty and the Lamb are the Temple and the Light thereof (Rev. 21:22-23); a place where there is no night (Rev. 22:5); and a place where we see the face of Christ (Rev. 22:4). It is there that Christ will change our lowly bodies that they might be fashioned like unto His glorious body, for there, we shall see Him as He is, for we shall be like Him (1 John 3:2).

St. Gregory of Sinai explains that

> [the] Kingdom of Heaven is like the tabernacle which was built by God, and which He disclosed to Moses as a pattern (Exod. 25:40); for it too has an outer and an inner sanctuary. Into the first will enter all who are priests of grace. But into the second—which is noetic—will enter only those who in this life have attained the divine darkness[10] of theological wisdom and there as true hierarchs have celebrated the triadic Liturgy, entering into the tabernacle that Jesus Himself has set up, where He acts as their consecrator and chief Hierarch before the Trinity, and illumines them ever more richly with His own splendor.[11]

---

[10] Divine darkness is an apophatic statement concerning the experience of God.

[11] *On Commandments and Doctrines,* 43, *Philokalia,* vol. 4, 220.

In heaven there are many dwellings (John 14:2) and different degrees of glory (1 Cor. 15:41) according to the purity and labors of each soul and the degree in which they partake of the one and the same uncreated energy of God. Yet "all of them shine in a single divine firmament."[12] The kingdom of heaven is not static, as man will forever be acquiring further gifts of grace and knowledge, with the longing for such blessings never abating. In eternity, no straying from virtue to vice is possible,[13] and man continues forever in the path which he has chosen in his life on earth.

There are indeed many accounts of saints who have experienced Paradise and have explained what they saw. Yet, while these accounts are good and beneficial, the higher and safer way in our pleasure-loving, self-seeking age is to remember rather the judgment of God and consider ourselves "unprofitable servants" as the Lord commands (Luke 17:10). The Orthodox Church focuses on repentance, with the concern of actualizing the kingdom in this world through virtue and God's grace: i.e., keeping the commandments, humbling oneself, being sober and temperate in all things, etc.

We recall that Christ first descended before He ascended. We too must descend with Christ into hell before we can properly experience heaven; that we may find divine humility through our voluntary self-emptying, making ourselves of no account, enabling the heart to become the habitation of the Holy Spirit.

On the other hand, it may be said that at times, there can be an overemphasis on hell. This may cause a reaction within

---

[12] Ibid., 221.
[13] Ibid., 222.

us which must be avoided. The remembrance of hell and death must be used as a medicine, in a measured quantity.

Elder Zacharias recommends that if we cannot "keep our mind in hell and despair not," we can most certainly give thanks to God for everything (1 Thes. 5:18). This not only is the will of God concerning us in Christ Jesus, but, according to St. Barsanuphius the Great, this also intercedes for our weaknesses:

> If we give ourselves over to the spirit of thanksgiving, God showers upon us even greater blessings. And there comes a point when we see God's providence everywhere we look ... [for] the spirit of thanksgiving [will] also lead man to repentance.[14]

It is through thanksgiving that we see all of God's benefits, revealing how often we are unaware of what has been given to us. In this way we develop a sense of contrition which leads us to repentance.

Heaven is not a place but a Person. It is personal communion with the Triune God and experiential knowledge of the Lord Jesus Christ, which is eternal Life (John 17:3). Hell is the loss or refusal of this communion, whether by our conscious rejection or the denial of it by our lives. The reality of heaven and hell is clearly taught throughout the Holy Scriptures, particularly by the Lord Jesus Christ Himself. It is only in the light of Orthodoxy that we come to know the full extent of the sobering reality of God's eternal love for mankind.

---

[14] (Zachariou), *Remember Thy First Love,* 292.

BEAUTY THAT SAVES THE WORLD: BEAUTY, LITURGY, AND LITURGICAL ART

CONCERNING THE ACCOUNT OF the Transfiguration of Christ as recorded in the Gospels, St. Gregory Palamas comments:

> ...in accordance with the Savior's promise, [the disciples] did see the kingdom of God, that divine and inexpressible light. St. Gregory of Nazianzos and St. Basil call this light "Divinity," saying that "the light is the divinity manifested to the disciples on the Mount,"[1] and that [this light] is "the beauty of Him Who is Almighty...." St. Basil ... said that this light is the beauty of God contemplated by the saints alone in the power of the divine Spirit....[2]

---

[1] St. Gregory Nazianzos, Oration 40:6 *PG* xxxvi, 365A, quoted in *Philokalia*, vol. 4, 415.

[2] St. Gregory Palamas, *Topics of Natural and Theological Sciences,* Ibid.

The heart of Orthodox Christian spirituality is the Incarnation of Jesus Christ. The Eternal *Logos*[3] became flesh (John 1:14) and restored creation's beauty which had become contra-natural, disfigured, and made ugly by sin. The restoration to the world of this archetypal beauty, which is Christ Himself, is the essential part of creation's redemption. The Church, as Christ's Body, incarnates this beauty into the world through her Liturgy, with its symphony of liturgical arts. As the new, transfigured, and restored creation, the Church provides windows for all to see and behold the glory of God, by which they can be sanctified. Being mystically called by and witnessing this beauty of Holiness,[4] we begin to participate in the deifying vision of God, which is salvation. To the degree that we participate in this eternal divine beauty is the extent that we actualize the beauty inherent in God's creative act; we ourselves become transfigured in the process and through it find salvation.

Salvation is our cooperative effort with God's grace through the keeping of the commandments and the acquisition of the beauty of the virtues, which bring man, who is in the image of God, to the likeness of God. As the summit of creation's beauty, St. John Chrysostom tells us that "there is nothing more beautiful than a beautiful soul...." He exhorts us therefore to "seek this beauty, in order that God might desire our beauty and impart to us the eternal blessings."[5]

---

[3] The *Logos* is the formative principle and reason behind all created things; it is Christ Himself. "All things were made by Him [Christ the *Logos*]" (John 1:3); "He is before all things, and in him all things hold together" (Col. 1:17 ESV).

[4] See Ps. 28:2, 95:9 LXX.

[5] St. John Chrysostom, "Homilies on St. Matthew" quoted in *Nicene*

The Life of Liturgy: The Church

The content of a transformed Christian life gives content to the liturgical art of the Church. Man, through the prayer, "Thy Kingdom come, Thy will be done," brings the Kingdom of God to his world, to the extent that he becomes like unto Christ through his effort and participation in the Life of the Holy Spirit. Through his repentance, man begins to actualize the Kingdom of God within himself; it begins to pour forth from him like a living fountain[6] which transfigures, sanctifies, and re-orders the entire world around him.

The liturgical art that exists within the traditional canonical[7] framework of the Church's life reflects and participates in this outpouring of the Kingdom into this world through the heart, mind, and body of the believer who has become part of Christ's Body. As man continues in his ascent to a greater communion with God, so too the world around him begins to be restored; it concurrently finds its transfiguration through its contact with the believer who is part of Christ's Body, just as Christ's clothing shone forth on Tabor through contact with His Body.

This restoration of man and his life takes place primarily through the transfiguring vision of God, which is noetic,[8]

---

and Post Nicene Fathers, vol. 10, trans. and ed. Philip Schaff (Grand Rapids: Eerdman's, 1975), 231.

[6] See John 7:38.

[7] Canonical means to abide within the boundaries established by the Holy Fathers of the Orthodox Church. It requires reception by the entire Church. Obedience to the canonical life of the Church enables us to abide in the Mind of Christ.

[8] Noetic, meaning relating to the nous. See page 15 of "Prayer as Communion" for the definition of nous.

taking place in the depths of the heart of man, encompassing every faculty of his body, mind, and soul, and embracing every aspect of his life. Through the sacramental-ascetical life of the Church, man can begin to see God in all things, at every moment, within and without, through the purity of his heart.[9] God is seen in and through Christ and His Church,[10] actively reconciling, transfiguring, and deifying it. Man, as the high priest of creation, works cooperatively with God through the canonical tradition and Liturgy of the Church in offering the creation back to the Creator.

The Church as the New Creation: A Second Paradise

The Scriptures teach us that Christ came to destroy death and him who had the power of death, that is, the devil,[11] the Prince of this world. Death, and its inseparable companion corruption, entered into all of creation at the time of the Fall; until now it groans, awaiting man's redemption.[12] Consequently, all of creation is called to, and needs to enter into, the Church, to be redeemed from the corruptive influences of fallen man and evil spirits who have brought about its disintegration.

The Church teaches us not only to be concerned with the salvation of our souls, but also of our bodies, and by extension the entire material world of which our bodies are part. Consequently, "by His incarnation Christ enthroned the whole of material creation on the throne of God: creation became the

---

9 See Matt. 5:8.

10 God is seen not in His essence but His energies.

11 See Heb. 2:14.

12 See Rom. 8:22.

flesh of the Word, and all the world became the Church."[13] The Incarnation and Resurrection of Christ raised up the "clay" of humanity to the very throne of God, deifying it like a fire unites with iron, remaining distinct without separation.

Thus, the Church's perspective is not dualistic,[14] but rather sees that the spiritual and material parts of man are both in need of transfiguration and redemption. Man is not saved without the body; through the body he has his being and life. Our quest is not a mental salvation that we seek in the Church through our thoughts about God; such thinking is rationalistic Scholastic theology and can result in a schism of soul and body, perverting our perception of reality. Rather, we need to transfigure our whole mind, body, and soul through a focus on repentance and the sacramental-ascetical life within the Church.

The creation by its very nature is good,[15] showing forth the eternal power of God.[16] The prophet Isaiah tells us that the angels sang before the throne of God the words: "Heaven and earth are full of Thy glory..." (Isa. 6:3). Similarly, the Prophet David exclaimed: "The heavens declare the glory of God..." (Ps. 18:1 LXX). Thus, the Church with her sacraments, artwork, and Liturgy, seeks to proclaim not only this power, but even more so the saving glory reinvested into the creation that comes through the Incarnation. It proclaims that,

---

[13] Christos Yannaras, *The Freedom of Morality*, trans. Elizabeth Briere (Crestwood: St. Vladimir's Seminary Press, 1984), 249.

[14] A teaching which states that the material world is inherently impure, and thus incompatible with the spiritual world.

[15] See Gen. 1.

[16] See Rom. 1:20.

consequently, salvation begins in, and through, this world *today*, and is not just an idea in the future world to come.

The vision of God's uncreated beauty and life in the creation is a vision of salvific beauty which is not in "a category of aesthetics" or an end in itself. Rather, beauty must be understood as "the divine grace and energy which forms and holds together the universe."[17] St. Paul in his second Epistle to the Corinthians explains that this vision of God's glory is at the heart of salvation. We are created in the image of God and called to participate in His likeness through the vision of this glory, for "we all, with open face beholding [or reflecting] as in a glass the glory of the Lord, are changed into the same image from glory to glory, even as by the Spirit of the Lord" (II Cor. 3:18).

It is precisely this deifying uncreated glory which is the "Kingdom of God, that divine and inexpressible light, [the light of Divinity which]… is 'the beauty of Him Who is Almighty….'"[18] For the Orthodox, this vision of the uncreated glory of God is the pinnacle of salvation throughout the Old and the New Testaments. Many are not granted the fullest participation in such a vision like St. Gregory Palamas and other saints. However, participation in the Church's liturgical life, when coupled with a life in obedience to the commandments of Christ and the Church's teachings, enables us to begin to partake of and behold the saving, deifying, and uncreated Beauty of God, no matter what our spiritual level.

---

[17] Archimandrite Vasileios, *Beauty and Hesychia in Athonite Life* (Montreal: Alexander Press, 1999), 10.

[18] St. Gregory Palamas, *Philokalia,* vol. 4, 415.

The Experience of God

Within the canonical framework of the Church, we might say that the experience or perception of God and His uncreated beauty can take place on many different levels and to varying degrees. Properly speaking, this experience is primarily within the inner heart of man, "for the Kingdom of God is within" (Luke 17:21). Yet, like Mary Magdalene, we too may hear the Lord's voice in the Gospel readings or the hymns of the Church and know that it is indeed our Lord. Or maybe, like Luke and Cleopas on the road to Emmaus, we will recognize Him clearly and strikingly in the breaking of the Bread, the Holy Eucharist, and our hearts will burn within us. Or maybe, like the sinful woman, we might sense a fragrant ointment of myrrh from our tears of repentance which are received by the Lord and poured out at His feet in the sacrament of Confession. All of these events, occurring within a sober and humble spiritual life, under the direction of a spiritual father, lead to the believer's personal participation in the saving energies of God.

St. Maximus the Confessor reminds us that the Holy Spirit is not absent from any part of creation, but is present in varying degrees:

> The Holy Spirit is not absent from any created being ... For being God and God's Spirit, He embraces in unity the spiritual knowledge of created things, providentially permeating all things

with His power, and vivifying their inner essences
in accordance with their nature.[19]

It is this presence of the Holy Spirit within the created order
that makes for creation's unique and innate *sacramentality*.
This gives the created world a potential that can be further
actualized by man's cooperative action with God through the
canonical traditions of the Church. Liturgical art becomes a
participant in the New Creation through the grace of the Holy
Spirit by virtue of the Incarnation of Christ.

Therefore, in our weakness, the Church assists us. As a
good Mother, the Church provides through her Liturgy and
her liturgical art the witness of the Kingdom among us. She
provides different "windows" that let in the rays of the Spirit,
illumining and healing our souls, granting us humble visions
into the inexpressible.

The Life of Prayer for All (1 Thes. 5:17): Stillness or Hesychia[20]

The Church's worship is reflective of her spiritual life and
dogma. And her spiritual life is reflected in her liturgical art.
Liturgical art can be a vessel that reveals and points to the
Church's incarnational vision, that "God is with us" (Isa. 8:10);
that the "middle wall of separation" (Eph. 2:14) between God
and man has been abolished. Liturgical art can be sacramental, a vessel of grace, capable of transmitting sanctification to
those who personally participate in the ascetic, liturgical, and
sacramental life of the Church.

---

[19] St. Maximus, *Philokalia,* vol. 2, 180.

[20] See page 2 for the definition of hesychia.

At the basis of this vision is the hesychastic understanding of prayer. Hesychasm is integral to the apostolic and Orthodox experience of prayer. The Church's teaching is clear: the ascetic, hesychastic, liturgical life of God is intended for all of God's people, since it facilitates the vision of God, which is salvation itself.

The hesychastic understanding of spiritual life, which has always been upheld in the Church, most concisely articulated by St. Gregory Palamas, is not a repression or dissolution of man and his passions. Rather, the hesychastic way leads to the transfiguration of man's fallen passions, and the reorientation of all his natural powers in a movement towards God. Basically, hesychasm is a way of anticipation and even a foretasting of the restoration of the created order. Orthodox spirituality and its liturgical art reflect this Life in Christ. It is not a spiritualization that ends in rejection and dissolution, but an acceptance, a liberation, and a reorientation of the world back to the source of Life, Who is Christ.

Since liturgical art reflects the theological vision of the Church, it is clear that if someone holds to erroneous theological teachings about God, they will have an improper view of His creation and therefore liturgical art. If the Incarnation did not occur and if God did not become man in the Person of Jesus Christ, then the material creation remains without hope for its ultimate renewal and regeneration in Christ.

The very heart of the Church's liturgical art is the restoration to creation of the beauty, perfection, and goodness which is natural to God. Within this theological perspective, beauty is not and cannot be subjective. Rather, beauty is objective Truth itself. Through liturgical art, man can personally participate in the Church's experience of God. Through the Incarnation, the human body and the matter of this world have now become "the Way" into the deifying vision of God.

It is therefore imperative to rid the mind of an "either/or" dualistic mentality towards the world. Creation is not bad; it was, and is, good, and the Holy Spirit is present within it, ordering and vivifying it. The Church affirms the world as indispensable. She therefore works not to eliminate it, but to purify it, to reorient it, and to offer it back to God.

The Orthodox teaching tells us that

> [creation has] a necessary role in the ascent of man to God…. On the road of our approach to God stands the world—we must pass through the understanding of it…. A mainly negative attitude toward the world frustrates salvation itself…. The world is a teacher to lead us to Christ. Of course it can also be the road to hell. It is the Tree of the Knowledge of Good and Evil, the tree of testing.[21]

Liturgical art in its manifold forms (especially iconography) is the Church's confirmation of the reality of the Incarnation of God into the matter of this world. The iconographic understanding of all of the Church's liturgical art is not based on philosophical or natural thought, which would simply give the fallen world 'religious meaning.' Rather, it is based on a *symbolic* understanding of the created world.

A symbol is defined by the Romanian theologian Dumitru Staniloae as a "visible reality which doesn't only represent but

---

[21] Dumitru Staniloae, *Orthodox Spirituality,* trans. Fr. Jerome Newville (South Canaan: St. Tikhon's Seminary Press, 2002), 205.

somehow makes an unseen reality visible."[22] We are reminded of St. Paul's understanding in Romans that this visible world serves as a mirror of God's invisible power and eternal Godhead.[23]

In contrast, the prevalent understanding in the secular world of today considers the world and man as being autonomous, and they remain intrinsically separated from God. This view is a product of the Enlightenment and Scholasticism and should be considered a modern heresy of the worst kind. It presents to us again the familiar image of man's Fall from Paradise: the world is used for man's own sake, apart from and separated from God, rather than as a means of communion and thanksgiving to God.

Unfortunately, this view undergirds life in most of our modern world, a fundamental error which begins with separating the thought of the created world from the thought of God. This can be seen as a product of the Scholastic mind that categorizes the world as "natural" and God and His grace as "supernatural;" it effectively erects a barrier in one's understanding of the created world and God, rendering the world, as Father Alexander Schmemann wrote, "grace-proof."[24]

We must accept in thought and reality the alliance of these two worlds, the spiritual and the material. We can see that the reality of the body and the soul reveals this concept. At the same time, we must grant the possibility that anything which

---

[22] Ibid., 205.

[23] See Rom. 1:20.

[24] Alexander Schmemann, *For the Life of the World* (Crestwood: St. Vladimir's Seminary Press, 1963), 130.

is before us, here and now, can bring together the spiritual and material, revealing something infinitely greater than itself.[25]

Within this understanding, we can begin to look at a few of the various forms of liturgical art and outline some basic conditions that must be met for them to be a genuine expression of the salvation of man and the world.

Concepts in Liturgical Art

Symbolism is an essential element of Orthodox spiritual life. The Church utilizes her symbolic art to heal our broken and torn reality, thereby restoring the diabolic breach between man and creation caused by the Fall. If in the Garden of Paradise the serpent's work was diabolic (*dia-bolos,* literally meaning 'tearing apart' of two things; e.g., reality and life), then in the Second Garden, the Church's liturgical work is symbolic (*sym-bolos,* literally meaning 'bringing two things together').

The symbolic aspect of the Church's art must be seen as a unification which ties the innate *sacramentality* of this world to the reality of the heavenly world. The symbolic aspect that by definition is present in liturgical art manifests the link between the spiritual and material. This tie was made into an indestructible reality through the Incarnation of Jesus Christ.

Consequently, the symbolic aspect of liturgical art is a manifestation of the Incarnation,

> [a] revelation, in and through Christ, of the "new Creation," and not the creation of something

---

[25] A symbol "by its very nature does not subject the infinite to the finite … but renders the finite transparent and allows us to see the infinite through it" (Staniloae, *Orthodox Theology,* 207).

new ... [for] if [the sacraments] reveal the continuity between the creation and Christ, it is
because there exists, at first, a continuity between
Christ and creation whose logos, life and light He
is.[26]

The manifestation of the new creation is not possible if a
second criterion is not observed and strictly adhered to: abiding in the *canonical* tradition of the Church. Whatever is done
within the Church is not haphazard, but is the result of the
mystical activity of the Holy Spirit within the Church, moving,
breathing, and living in Her members; this is the essence of
Holy Tradition. The canonical statutes that govern liturgical
art, whether written or unspoken, are an imperative necessity.
This canonical fellowship with the Church guarantees the fellowship with the Holy Trinity.[27]

The canonical tradition is not necessarily written; it is
rather the transference of the Church's mind and life from one
person to another. All that has come before is an invaluable
asset to understanding how to proceed today in a traditional
and canonical way. It might be said that the liturgical services
themselves, when done lovingly, carefully, and humbly, day
in and day out (especially in the monastic context), give the
instruction that we need to guide us into the way which is
fitting, traditional, and canonical. However, there are only
a few canons dictating the "how to" of canonical art; therefore it is imperative that we receive formation in liturgical art.
This formation is given to us by those who have mastery of
an area of canonical art which is in continuity with tradition

---

[26] Schmemann, *For the Life of the World,* 144.

[27] See 1 John 1:3.

and accepted by the Church.[28] Through obedience to those
who have this good witness, we imperceptibly gain the Mind
of Christ. Joined with spiritual disciplines such as prayer and
fasting, we can be illumined to a fuller understanding of what
can be considered canonical; that in due time, just by hearing
or looking at different manifestations of liturgical art, we can
discern what is true and right. Through this, it is possible to
become, as many monastics have in the past, living *typicons*.[29]

Canonical art is the expression of authentic spiritual vision
beyond the perceptible natural world. Tradition defines the
parameters that can artistically incarnate this vision of truth.
Thus, the Church's icons serve to give the "reason" (*logos*) to
form and material, giving an entrance into the spiritual world.
The prototypes for icons and canonical traditions in hymnography are not by chance, but are given by the saints who
have seen and heard what has "never entered into the heart of
man" (1 Cor. 2:9), and which is not "lawful for a man to utter"
(II Cor. 12:4). As an example, we often think of the story of
the hymnographer St. Romanos the Melodist. After having a
vision of the Mother of God, St. Romanos entered the Church
and began singing, under divine inspiration, what we know
today as the *kontakion* for the Nativity of Christ.

The prototypes for hymns and icons are a "visible image
of mysterious supernatural vision."[30] This vision manifests the

---

[28] No one learns liturgical art by oneself. A new priest learns from an
experienced liturgist. An aspiring iconographer learns from a master. A new
choir director learns from an experienced professional.

[29] The *typicon* is the Church's rulebook for liturgical life.

[30] St. Dionysius the Areopagite, quoted from Pavel Florensky, *Iconostasis,*
trans. Donald Sheehan and Olga Andrejev (Crestwood: St. Vladimir's Seminary Press, 1996), 65.

"spotless archetypes[31] by means of which the divine [content] … of the Christian religion becomes apparent and palpable to the senses."[32] Through this vision, we enter into the unity of mind we find in the saints, known as the 'dogmatic visionary consciousness.'

By embracing this consciousness, we reject the fragmented, self-enclosed individualism that gropes for truth. Through this embrace, we find a freedom of expression in the canonical patterns of art that manifest and bless the uniquely personal aspects of each artist. At the same time, this embrace affirms the unity that overcomes the fragmentation of the world, restoring communion with God in the Body of Christ. As a modern commentator notes,

> The artist who bases his work on the canonical tradition (if it can be found where he is) discovers in and through the canons the energy to create works…. To accept the traditional canon is to enter into a relationship with all humanity and to realize that humanity has not lived in vain, that it has not been without truth, and that, instead, it has comprehended truths that have been tested and purified by the councils and the generations; thus, humanity is confirmed in the canons.[33]

---

[31] An archetype is the reality on which imitations are based. For example, the earthly Divine Liturgy is based on and participates in the archetype of the heavenly Divine Liturgy as seen in Rev. 4-5.

[32] Photios Kontoglou, *Byzantine Sacred Art* (Belmont: Institute for Byzantine and Modern Greek Studies, 1985), 126.

[33] Florensky, *Iconostasis*, 80.

We should therefore define canonical art not just as a set of rules and regulations (although it can mean that), but rather the life of the Church, manifested and transmitted from person to person encounters, which ultimately leads back to Christ and the apostles. This happens as well as through the liturgical life of the Church: her prayers, her feasts, her fasts, the Eucharist, etc. It is only in this daily rhythm of the life of the Church, coupled with study of the history of the Church's theological and artistic past, that we can carefully discern the real content of canonicity for liturgical art and life.

Having established that Orthodox liturgical art must be canonical and symbolic, we must consider another facet: the iconic level. Whether music, icons, or architecture, the central goal of iconic reality must be fulfilled: to lead from the image to the archetype, from the earthly to the heavenly.

Many primitive peoples today refuse to have their photograph taken by a camera. The reason is simple: their understanding is that the picture takes part of their soul away. This illustrates a simple but a profound reality which concerns iconic art. Iconic art is understood as the depiction of the nature of things and people themselves, not by imitation, but by the revelation of its deeper spiritual reality.

The Incarnation of Christ and the Descent of the Holy Spirit are the bridge between the two worlds, heaven and earth, that once were separated by the Fall. This is exemplified best by the teachings given in the Church hymnography for the Sunday of the Triumph of Orthodoxy:[34]

---

[34] The Sunday of Orthodoxy is the triumph of the veneration of icons as defined by the Seventh Ecumenical Council of 787.

The uncircumscribed[35] Word of the Father became circumscribed, taking flesh from thee, O Theotokos, and He has restored the sullied image to its ancient glory, filling it with the divine beauty. This, our salvation, we confess in deed and word and we depict it in the holy icons.[36]

The restoration of, and the actualization of, the glory, grace and beauty inherent in creation was brought about in Christ. The icon confirms that it is indeed this world that Christ joined to His incorruptible Godhead. By venerating the image of Christ, we recognize that the icon is the beginning of the vision of God: "the knowledge of the glory of God in the face of Jesus Christ" (II Cor. 4:6). The third canon of the Council of 867 emphatically affirmed what it means to go against this principle: "If one does not venerate the icon of Christ the Savior, let him not see His Face at the Second Coming."[37] The veneration of the image is the beginning of, and a pledge of, the vision of God. It is the beginning and continuation of the fellowship with Him Who was seen, Who was heard, Who was handled; of the very Word of Life Himself. Christ is the restoration of that beauty that was lost at the Fall; the beauty which man had by God's grace and into which he was intended to grow.

Likewise, the canonical hymns of the Church provide another means for us to hear the voice of Christ, transforming the deepest places of our hearts, accessible through music. These

---

[35] Uncircumscribed, meaning without limit; cannot be confined.

[36] *The Lenten Triodion,* Kontakion on Ode 6, Sunday of Orthodoxy. trans. Mother Mary and Kallistos Ware (South Canaan: St. Tikhon's Seminary Press, 2002), 306.

[37] Leonid Ouspensky, *Theology of the Icon* (Crestwood: St. Vladimir's Seminary Press, 1992), 213.

hymns "are the reflection of the spiritual chants, transmitted by the celestial hierarchy [i.e., angels] to mankind and made audible to human ears in the form of Psalms." By following the canonical and iconic models, we hear "an echo of the hymn sung by the angels in His praise," for "the vast treasury of Byzantine [canonical] melodies was developed from a limited number of archetypes, transmitted by the angels to prophets and inspired saints. Thus the heavenly hymns became perceptible to human ears."[38]

It is possible, according to St. Dionysius,[39] that through these hymns we can be led to the archetypes of the angelic hymns. If sacred music is to fulfill the end for which it is employed, it must facilitate this ascent from the material to the spiritual. Similar to the icon, it must go from the image to the prototype. When seen as a sacramental vessel of grace, the Church's music has an equal part in helping man towards theosis;[40] towards knowing God and fulfilling His will. Touching the deepest places of man's being, the Church's hymnography calls forth a change from deep within: to a greater love, a greater effort, and a greater repentance. At an iconic level, hymnography is a participation and a "vision" of the beauty of holiness, "seen" inside the heart of man. Mankind, in chorus with angels, lauds God's plan of salvation in Christ, ultimately leading us back to the throne of God, where all harmony and beauty have their beginning and ending.

Thus, within the polyphony of liturgical sight and sound, the Church's transformative movement in this world

[38] Egon Wellesz, *Byzantine Music and Hymnography* (London: Oxford University Press, 1971), 59-60.

[39] St. Dionysius the Aeropagite, *Ecclesiastical Hierarchy,* 3:4-7.

[40] See page 30 for the definition of theosis.

ultimately orients everything back to the Eucharist. The new creation of liturgical art is Eucharistic, a united hymn of praise and thanksgiving, with Christ becoming all in all. We, being joined to Him, are restored from death to life through partaking of His divine Body and Blood. The Church exists for the Eucharist: the marriage of the Bride, the Church, with her Bridegroom, Christ. This perfect union is seen in every detail within the Church, which facilitates this process by calling everyone, and everything, to enter into the marriage feast, the union between God and man.

The Church building is a canonical icon, housing the new creation in Christ; an icon which has its unity not on a drawing board from the mind of man, but rather in the Mind of Christ. Its scheme of iconography, hymnography, and architecture reflects the vision of the entirety of Life in Christ. It is a vast symphony of the sights, sounds, and beauties of heaven which illumines, heals, guides, comforts, and deifies us.

Christos Yannaras summarizes that

> [Within the Church is] the entire heavenly and earthly creation, destined to become a new creation in Christ the God-Man, [which] is gathered around Christ in the dome and around Mary in the apse. The angelic powers, mankind, animals, the birds, the plants, and the stars—the entire universe unites to form an unmatched temple of God (heavenly and earthly in harmony). The entire world is sheltered under the vault of the

Church; this is an image of unity restored, the
unity that was broken by the fall of man.[41]

In conclusion, we must begin to recognize the Church as
our Fathers teach: it is the Second Paradise, having within
its midst that Tree of Life, the Cross, which has blossomed
forth its fruit for the world, the Eucharist: Christ Himself. The
canonical liturgical tradition is the incarnation of heaven in
earth through the God-Man, Jesus Christ. The liturgical tradition presupposes a worldview which embraces this Mind of
Christ; one which is mystical and ascetical. Liturgical art is
ascetical; it is sacramental; and it is capable of transmitting
grace to those who are properly disposed, initiating them into
the vision of Christ through His Church. The sacred beauty
that we perceive through liturgical art is the beauty of holiness that sanctifies, nourishes, and produces growth in the
hearts, bodies, and minds of those who have eyes to see and
ears to hear. To see and hear implies a constant participation
in the sacramental-ascetical and liturgical life of the Church;
a narrow way and a continuous struggle which acclimatizes
one to the very life and rhythm of heaven; a new and eternal
life which has a beginning in this world today, but one which
never ends throughout all eternity.

---

[41] Yannaras, *The Freedom of Morality*, 222.

MONASTICISM: ANCIENT AND CONTEMPORARY VALUES OF A TIMELESS TRADITION

MONASTIC LIFE IS AN ENIGMA to the modern world. Oftentimes, even those in the Church are led to wonder what such a life as monasticism is 'worth.' What does it do? What kind of product does it have to give to the world? However, monasticism is intimately linked with the essence of Christianity. If we really embrace Who Jesus Christ is and how we are called to His likeness, then understanding the role of monasticism will be inevitable. The monastic life is nothing less than one hundred percent Christianity, one hundred percent of the time. It is the epitome of the Gospel message lived to its fullest extent.

A life of dedicated prayer and asceticism predates the Christian Church. In the Old Testament, we see monastic life prefigured, such as in the life of the Prophet Elijah. In the New Testament, monasticism is epitomized, of course, by St. John the Baptist. Living in solitary seclusion on whatever means the wilderness provided, St. John provides an image and model for all those who would follow a life dedicated to prayer and fasting.

St. Paul the Apostle speaks at length in his Epistles of this radically different way of life, but also reveals its deeply Christian character:

> It is good for a man not to touch a woman. Nevertheless, to avoid fornication, let every man have his own wife, and every woman have her own husband.... To the unmarried and widows, it is good for them if they abide even as I. But if they cannot contain themselves, let them marry.... I would that all men were even as I myself [i.e., unmarried].... He that is unmarried cares for the things that belong to the Lord, and how he may please the Lord, but he that is married cares for the things that are of the world and how he may please his wife (1 Cor. 7:1-2, 8-9, 7, 32-33).

In St. Paul's time, there were many who consecrated themselves to a life of virginity or abstaining from marriage, such as the houses of widows that were spoken of by St. Paul and other early Fathers. Even before this time, we see those who stayed praying and serving in the Temple, such as St. Anna the Prophetess and St. Symeon the God-receiver, who met the Lord in the Temple.

So, even early in the history of the New Testament, we have many examples of monastic life. Because most of these early Christians faced the constant peril of martyrdom, their level of commitment was unique: it was total and complete.

Under St. Constantine the Great, Christianity became a legal religion for the general population, resulting in a less intense and committed expression of Christian faith. Christians such as St. Anthony the Great and St. Pachomius the Great continued to desire to follow the way of radical and total commitment to the Gospel of Christ. The struggles, perils, and temptations of the first centuries of the Church formed the crucible in which Christianity became what it actually is: the abundant life that Christ promised to the disciples,[1] a life of total and uncompromising commitment to Christ, and to the narrow way of the Cross. Those who first went out into the desert, and became the first monks and nuns, were none other than those who sought after this same abundant life in Christ.

The Cross itself is the best example of this abundant life that Christ offers His disciples: Either you crucify yourself with Christ, or you do not. This is our constant struggle today, whether we are married or monastic. Each day we have to recommit to following Christ. Each moment we are offered choices which test us as to our disposition: Will we follow Christ, or ourselves and the world? The level of commitment that is required of monastics is no different from those who are married. Our marital status is not the issue. Rather, for us, the concern is the disposition of our hearts and the willingness we have to follow the Lord.

Monasticism is often distasteful to many in the modern world. Essentially it is a reminder, and indeed an icon, of another world and another way of life. The life of monasticism challenges us all, no matter who we are.

Monasticism is an attempt to abandon one's own will, so that God's will and providence (that is, whatever He sends) may lead us toward our ultimate salvation. The Fall of

---

[1] See John 10:10.

mankind away from God is essentially a corruption of the will of man, making it difficult to choose what is right and pleasing in God's sight. Monastics strive to harmonize their will with God's will so that they might begin to reenter the Kingdom of God, even while still in this world. This connection between the Kingdom and God's will is revealed in the Lord's Prayer: "Thy Kingdom come, Thy will be done, on earth as it is in heaven."

Monasticism is not about obeying a commandment or fulfilling an injunction, but rather it is acting on a voluntary evangelic calling. It was said to the man who told the Lord that he had done everything possible in the service of God: "If you want to be perfect, go and sell all that you have … and you will have treasure in heaven: and come and follow me" (Matt. 19:21). Further, the proscription to abstain from marriage was only said by the Lord "to whom it has been given" (Matt. 19:11). Monasticism is clearly a calling from God, unique and unrepeatable for each person called to that life.

The life of monastics shows that this abundant life in Christ is actually to be found only in death: that is, death to the passions, the sins, and the lusts that attempt to possess us. This is ultimately revealed by the Cross of Christ, which teaches us that death for the sake of God's will and His commandments brings true life. Our suffering is not pointless but can be redemptive if it is voluntarily accepted with faith in God's never-ending providential care for us.

Since monasticism seems highly impractical to the world and doesn't fit society's criteria of 'productivity,' it is easy to discount it when taken at a superficial level. In fact, the main work of monasteries is not to make jelly and candles, but rather to ceaselessly pray for the salvation of all mankind, both the living and the dead. This kind of prayer for mankind is of inestimable worth. However, this worth is not usually seen nor even quantifiable. Elder Sophrony of Essex writes,

> The Prophet Moses prayed and delivered the people of Israel from destruction. St. Anthony aided the world by his prayers, not by his handicraft nor his money. St. Sergius of Radonezh fasted and prayed, helping to liberate the Russian people from the Tatars' yoke. St. Seraphim of Sarov prayed silently and the Holy Spirit descended on his longtime friend and helper, Motovilov. This is the task of the monastic.[2]

Furthermore, St. Silouan the Athonite explained that this kind of prayer keeps the world going, and that when real prayer fails, the world will perish. He reiterated that when there are no more men of prayer on earth the world will come to an end.[3]

The life of monasticism is an icon of the kingdom which is present among us, and yet is to come. It reveals the commitment that every Christian everywhere should be making to God, no matter what their vocation or work. Monastics exemplify that faith which is the "substance of things hoped for, the evidence of things not seen" (Heb. 11:1), reminding us as Christians that "here we have no continuing city, but seek the one to come" (Heb. 13:14). Monasticism is the proof that Christianity is not only real, but that it really works. It is proof

---

[2] Archimandrite Sophrony (Sakharov), *St. Silouan the Athonite* (Essex: Monastery of St. John the Baptist, 1991), 408.

[3] See *St. Silouan the Athonite,* 223.

that man can find true peace in Christ when he wholeheart-edly submits to God's will and forsakes his own.

The model for monastics is none other than our Lord, God, and Savior: Jesus Christ. Monastics aim to imitate Christ, Whose way of life was altogether monastic. Metropolitan Hilarion Alfeyev writes, "[Christ] was not married; He was free from earthly bonds; He had no roof over His head, trav-eling from place to place; He lived in poverty; He fasted; He spent nights in prayer."[4] Christ is why monastics unsparingly follow the universal call to become like Christ.

Consequently, we must categorically affirm that monasti-cism is not a rejection of the material world, but rather a rejec-tion of the passions and lusts that corrupt it. This injunction of rejection of 'the world' in this sense is given to all Christians everywhere in St. John's First Epistle:

> Love not the world ... for all that is in the world,
> [i.e.,] the lust of the flesh, and the lust of the eyes,
> and the pride of life, is not of the Father.... The
> world passes away, and the lusts thereof, but he
> that does the will of God abides forever (1 John
> 2:15-17).

We know and understand that at the creation of the world, God looked upon it and said that it was good. Adam and Eve in the Garden had an ascetic command: to fast from the Tree of the Knowledge of Good and Evil. Only when they broke the fast, misusing the creation, did they find themselves sep-arated from God. Therefore, it is not the creation that is to be rejected but the misuse of it, just as it is not food which is bad,

---

[4] Alfeyev, *Mystery of Faith,* 158.

but gluttony; it is not money that is evil, but greed for it. This ascetic ethos of the Church applies equally for all people and is exemplified in monasticism.

The ascetical life is one of the central keys to understanding the deep mystery of the Christian faith. Just as the Cross is the heart of our salvation, so asceticism lies at the heart of the life of the Church. Asceticism *is* our Cross. To reject asceticism is to reject Christ, Who commands us to carry our Cross on the narrow way. Asceticism is the door to life with God.

The Church calls us to fast on Wednesdays and Fridays as well as during the four fasting periods of the year. This is not because there is something wrong with food and drink. Rather, there is something wrong with us that needs to be healed within our hearts. Wise and temperate fasting not only heals our passions, but it also helps us to appreciate what we have, enabling us to give thanks to God. Asceticism restores the connection of this world back to the Creator.

Monasticism constantly reminds the world of this need for an ascetical way of life. If we are to make spiritual progress, we must not, and cannot, constantly give in to whatever we want, whenever we want it. Monastics who fast show us that man is not dependent "on bread alone" (Matt. 4:4) but on God, the Creator and Giver of the bread. Monastics reveal that it is God's power that sustains us and not creation itself. This disproves the modern secular belief that disconnects this world from God and which depicts the world as something autonomous from Him.

The ascetical ethos of the Orthodox Church is precisely what has been removed from modern Christianity. We have forgotten this critical key in the pursuit of the new Life in Christ. However, it is this ascetical ethos, exhibited *par excellence* by monasticism, that restores a correct worldview, reconnecting it with God and placing it in its proper perspective. This effort is tireless and fought for until our last breath. However, through it, and because of it, when we leave this world, our heart's desire will not be for that which perishes and cannot be possessed after our death. This would only leave us eternally dissatisfied. If we desire goodness, love, and the Lord Himself; if we carry these things in our hearts; and if they become the content of our life, we will most certainly be in eternal rest in the Kingdom of God in the world to come. For "the Kingdom of God is not food and drink, but righteousness, peace, and joy in the Holy Spirit" (Rom. 14:17).

The life of monasticism, as a part of its restorative renunciation of the world, demands a vow of chastity. This is not a perversion of human nature as the world might argue. Rather, it is a regeneration and re-dedication of all human desire, energy, and power, so that it can be redirected towards love for God and the Kingdom of heaven. A monastic is not married to an earthly spouse but to a Heavenly One. The relationship is not physical, but spiritual, revealing a transcendental depth to human love that is possible for all.

Monasticism is not a rejection of marriage. Those who reject marriage are condemned by the Church's canons. Monastics seek something greater than mere celibacy: they embrace chastity, in Greek *sophrosyne,* literally meaning "wisdom" and "integrity." In monasticism, celibacy is only an element of chastity.[5] Chastity as wisdom and integrity leads to a life in accordance with the Gospel, abstaining from carnal passions and lusts. Metropolitan Hilarion writes, "To live in chastity

---

[5] See Alfeyev, *Mystery of Faith,* 160.

means to have one's entire life oriented to God, to check every thought, word and deed against the Gospel's standards."[6]

Chastity is indeed an imperative for marriage as well. Marriage entails remaining monogamous and faithful to one's spouse; attempting to refrain from sexual relations during the fasting periods; and even to refrain from looking with objectifying lust upon one another, even in thought or intention.

Monastics, though celibate, are alone but not lonely. They remain separate from all, and yet through this, by prayer and communion with God, they become united with all. Monasticism is not the opposite of marriage but rather a different kind of marriage, one that is between a human person and God Himself:

> Love is at the very heart of both marriage and monasticism, but the object of the love is different. A person cannot become a monk unless his love for God is so deep and ardent that he does not want to direct [it] towards anyone but [God].[7]

Consequently, some may think monastics are self-centered and self-serving individuals. This is typically far from the truth. Monastics still live in community life; for them, it is family. By accepting obedience to the abbot or abbess, and by attempting to cut off his will in community life, a monastic learns to accept within himself the will and the life of his monastic family. While at prayer, he bears in his heart the entire community; through this he begins to ascend from the "I" of self to the "we" of humanity. Elder Zacharias states,

---

[6] Ibid.
[7] Ibid.

He begins to experience humanity's pain and its eternal destiny as a matter of burning personal concern. And thus monasticism becomes the place where one can be introduced into the very life of Christ, one which embraces the totality of all humanity in time, space, and eternity.[8]

The monastic reminds everyone that the passions are not to be repressed but rather redirected. Whenever we encounter a temptation or a sinful passion, it is a call to prayer, and an opportunity to transform our energies and channel them into positive and life-giving alternatives. It is amazing that the short prayer, "Lord Jesus Christ, Son of God, have mercy on me," has the power to destroy the nets of the evil one and to subdue and change our passions. In fact, a foundation of a sinful life is the forgetfulness of God. When we remember God, it is this remembrance that breaks the power and strength of sin in our life.

Monasteries are abodes of this constant remembrance of God. They are places of ceaseless prayer. Just by visiting them for a day, our sinful tendencies can be curtailed, even rooted out. To visit a monastery is to visit a healing oasis of life, one which is permeated with God's healing grace and power. Monasteries flood an otherwise arid and barren world with this grace, causing a profound change in the spiritual atmosphere of the entire world. Those within the world are sometimes so busy that they either forget to pray or do not have the time to do so, while monasteries make it their main task, no matter what else they might produce to make a living.

---

[8] (Zachariou), *Christ, Our Way and Our Life*, 131.

Monasticism and marriage are not to be seen in opposition to each other but as two sides of the same Cross. Not all are called to marriage and family life and not all are called to live as monastics. However, we are all called to the same fullness of the life in Christ.

St. John Chrysostom reveals the true transcendental character of monasticism as a model for all Christians when he explains:

> You certainly deceive yourself and are greatly mistaken if you think that there is one set of requirements for the person in the world and another for the monk. The difference between them is that one is married and the other is not; in all other respects they will have to render the same account … For all people must reach the same point: [the full measure of Christ; to become perfect as the Father in heaven is perfect]. And this is what throws everything into disorder—the idea that only the monk is required to show a greater perfection, while the rest are allowed to live in laxity. But this is not true![9]

The Lord's own injunction in the Scriptures is clear: "Be ye holy, for I am holy" (1 Pet. 1:16).

As Christians we are all called to follow the same commandments; we are called to the same life of sacrifice, and a willingness to be crucified so that we can truly live with Christ and in Christ. In either state, married or monastic, we are

---

[9] St. John Chrysostom, *Against the Opponents of the Monastic Life,* III trans. by David Hunter (Edwin Mellen Press, 1988), 156-58.

called to sacrifice and die to ourselves. We all must endure some form of martyrdom. Both roads lead to the same Kingdom. Both can lead to holiness. The key is, as with everything in life, our disposition. Do we wish to please ourselves or the Lord? Is God first, or are we? In marriage, we die to ourselves and to our passions for the sake of our spouse. This martyrdom is referred to in the marriage service as we sing the hymn, "O holy martyrs, who fought the good fight and have received your crowns…."

The monastic takes vows of poverty, chastity, and obedience. We have already spoken about how chastity is to be attained and maintained in either the married or monastic state. Poverty in the married state is exhibited by stewardship of our time, our talents, and our resources (whether monetary or otherwise) to the Church and to those in need. Obedience is lived out in the married life through obedience to the Church's teachings and to her way of life, as well as obedience to the bishop, one's spiritual father, and obedience to one's spouse.

It is obvious that monastic and married lives are very different, and yet, there is only one model for all: our Lord Jesus Christ.

Many are called by God to the married life, living a godly, holy life, and raising God-fearing children to grow into good Orthodox Christians. This is an important calling. Likewise, some are called to the monastic life which is in imitation of the life of angels. Monastics strive to live a life, with the help of God's grace, as an image of the world to come. In either case, whether in marriage or monasticism, we must be faithful to what God has called us to.

It is often heard that monasticism is the barometer of the Church, and that the state of the Church's monastic life reveals its health and maturity. In many Orthodox countries, the monastery is seen as a center for the Church, a front line in the spiritual battle, forging the spiritual way for the greater Church community in a given area, bringing God's blessing, protection, and constant help to its inhabitants.

Unfortunately, monasticism does not currently have the same importance or support in American Orthodoxy. Today in Western society, the monastery is seen as something extra, an option, and not something central and fundamental to the life of the Church. Even worse, monasticism may be seen as an aberration, or something that is to be marginalized. Supporting our local monasteries with our time, talents, and resources shows that we value the growth of our Orthodox Church in America. We should never discourage anyone, whether a friend, a child, or a parent, from pursuing a potential monastic vocation. Personal and corporate growth within the parish and the support of monasteries are intertwined and inseparably bound.

Sainted monastics fill our Church calendars. They line the walls of our temples. They formulated and preserved not only the Church's doctrine, but also the treasury of the Church's liturgical life. Monastics were even the first to bring Orthodox Christianity to the New World in 1794. St. Herman of Alaska, St. Juvenaly the Protomartyr, and several other monks were the first to arrive on the shores of Alaska to begin the work of spreading the Orthodox Faith to this New Land. It was this first group of monastics which, through prayer and fasting and total commitment to Christ, converted thousands of Alaskans, paving the way for St. Innocent of Alaska in the 1840's to continue working the fields which had been planted, ripe for the harvest.

We, as members of Christ's Body, can and must support the building and growth of monasteries and monastic vocations. By so doing, we invest in the well-being and preservation of the Church as well as in the "churching" of America. Through the monasteries, organic Orthodox life will grow and flourish, and serving as a catalyst, will empower and inspire local parishioners to give more of their own hearts and lives to God. The spiritual power that emanates from a monastery is real, tangible, and intensely transformative.

The monastery sanctifies not only the monastics and those who visit but even the trees, the rocks, and the very ground itself. Often have we heard the expression "holy ground." This statement is not unfounded. As Christ's garments shone during the Transfiguration, so we know that the material world, when it comes into contact with Christ's Body, the Church, is illumined with grace. It is said that this kind of sanctification affects the whole universe, and when saints emerge from these habitations, in an unfathomable and yet real way, they become a catalyst for the salvation of nations and the entire material universe in which they live. May we strive, by the grace of God, to do the same.

ADAM, THE FIRST-CREATED MAN

THE THINGS OF THIS WORLD, when separated from God, deceptively promise fulfillment in the heart that they are incapable of delivering. They are created from nothing; their source is God's creative energy ("He spoke, and it came to be" [Ps. 33:9 LXX]). Consequently, it is God Who is the fulfillment for which the heart longs. Man's intuitive and innate search for fulfillment in the created world is inevitably a search for Paradise: Communion with God. In the quest for the fulfillment of life's goals, people tend to have a common underlying motivation whether they are conscious of it or not: the acquisition of a perceived "Paradise."

The account of Adam and Eve in the Holy Scriptures tells of a state in which the first-created man had communion with God, but was deceived, and lost communion through his own free choice. We will briefly explore some aspects of the biblical-patristic view of the reality of the first-created man, Adam; how he affects us, and how we can return to Eden through the Second Adam, the Lord Jesus Christ.

Before one can properly examine the biblical-patristic context for understanding the Genesis account of man in the Garden, one must first be open to consider several factors.

Unfortunately, the modern intellectual mind has an exceedingly difficult time in discerning the truth concerning the reality of the account of Adam in the Garden. To revisit Paradise ourselves, we must utilize other venues to understand the biblical account instead of preconceived notions and biased modern conceptions. Consequently, one must enter into a different level of perception, one which is in harmony with the vision that has been held in common for thousands of years by the faith which has received, held, and seen the Truth, living in the midst of the presence of the Lord God of Sabaoth: the Orthodox Church.

In seeking those things which are above, of course, one must not presume to be able to encompass the whole truth with the intellect, for this is the height of madness. St. Maximus the Confessor tells us "that the human intellect is not unaffected by man's [present] corrupt and mortal nature…" for the intellect "shares in and so also suffers from the present corruptibility of the human body."[1] Let us then wisely begin by looking to those who have had experience concerning the Mysteries of God, the confirmed and "sure word of prophecy" (II Pet. 1:19), looking to the miraculous unity of their vision for a way into the highest Truth: revelation, a confirmable knowledge that is by faith through God's Grace.

Equally important when studying the origin of man is to recognize the bearing our beliefs have on our lives and actions. The question of Adam as the first man created by God is not trivial but rather a central one concerning the question of

---

[1] Christopher Veniamin, "The Transfiguration of Christ and the Deification of Man in St. Maximus the Confessor," *The Orthodox Understanding of Salvation* (Dalton: Mount Thabor Publishing, 2014), 116.

salvation. If someone believes that we are created in the image of God, they will inevitably live and treat people differently than if they think that the world, and those around them, are a result of spontaneous chance springing from primordial chaos.

Every man must have a father. Logic will tell us that everything has a beginning. Thus, having the genealogical account in the Gospel of Luke which lists Christ's lineage from the first Adam to the Second Adam, it would be a strange inconsistency to consider the first Adam to be a non-existent allegory. If one calls into question the reality of the first-created man, it would not be long before the validity and necessity of the Second Adam, Christ, would also come into question, for they are inseparably interdependent.[2]

Amazingly, the Jewish people have always been absolutely meticulous concerning their genealogies. We thus might even dare to think that the account of Adam in the Garden is so simplistic that it might become confusing to our 'modern advanced intellectual prowess.' We, too, might be beguiled: "as the serpent beguiled Eve through his subtlety, so [our] minds should be corrupted from the simplicity that is in Christ" (II Cor. 11:3).

---

[2] "If any of us does not recognize he is Adam, the one who sinned before God in Paradise, how can he recognize and think that the coming down of the Son and Word of God was for him? … Just as each of us is Adam, that is, a corruptible and mortal man, not by reason of our own sin, but by reason of the disobedience of our first ancestor, Adam, from whose seed we come; so each of us is of Christ, immortal and incorrupt, not for the sake of our own virtues, but for the sake of the obedience of the Second Adam, Who is Christ our Lord…" (St. Symeon the New Theologian, Homily 38:1, quoted from *The First-Created Man: Seven Homilies by St. Symeon the New Theologian,* trans. Seraphim Rose [Platina: St. Herman of Alaska Brotherhood, 2013]).

To rightly begin, we must first see and understand that the Genesis account is a book of prophecy. St. John Chrysostom explains that

> all the other prophets spoke of what was to occur after a long time or of what was about to happen; but he, the blessed [Moses], who lived many generations after [the creation of the world], was vouchsafed by the guidance of the right hand of the Most High to utter what had been done by the Lord before his own birth … therefore I entreat you, let us pay heed to these words as if we heard not Moses but the very Lord of the universe Who speaks through the tongue of Moses, and let us take leave for good of our own opinions.[3]

Consider also St. Paul's vision of Paradise (II Cor. 12:2-4). St. Ambrose of Milan asks us concerning Paradise:

> [If it] is of such a nature that Paul alone, or one like Paul, could scarcely see it while alive, and was unable to remember whether he saw it in the body or out of the body … if this is true, how will it be possible for us to declare the position of Paradise which we have not been able to see? … The subject of Paradise should not then be treated lightly.[4]

---

[3] St. John Chrysostom, *The Fathers of the Church Patristic Series: Homilies on Genesis 1-17, 2:2*, trans. Robert Hill (Washington DC: Catholic University of America Press, 1999).

[4] St. Ambrose of Milan, *Hexameron, Paradise, and Cain and Abel*, trans. John Savage (Washington DC: Catholic University Press, 1961), 288.

St. Ephraim the Syrian and St. Gregory of Nyssa explain that Paradise belongs to another level of reality, not situated in time and space, but enveloping this world and yet transcending it. St. John of Damascus tells us that it was "a site higher in the East than all the earth...."[5] Therefore, St. Ephraim says,

> you should not let your intellect be disturbed by
> names, for Paradise [in the Genesis account] has
> simply clothed itself in terms that are akin to you
> ... your nature is far too weak to be able to attain
> to its greatness....[6]

Recall that even St. Mary Magdalene, when she first saw the Lord after His Resurrection, didn't recognize Him except by hearing His voice (John 20:16). In the case of Ss. Luke and Cleopas, Christ was known in the breaking of bread (Luke 24:35). Why might this be so? St. John Chrysostom answers with a question: "Has anyone ever seen a resurrected body?" Of course not; no one had until the time of the Lord Jesus Christ's Resurrection, and then only for forty days. If they could not then recognize the resurrected Lord Who from the Cross went to Paradise with the thief (Luke 23:43), how can we easily philosophize, without assistance, or be overly presumptuous concerning the present mystery of the Garden of Eden?

---

[5] St. John of Damascus, *Exact Exposition of the Orthodox Faith,* 29, quoted from *Nicene and Post Nicene Fathers,* vol. 7.

[6] St. Ephraim the Syrian, *Hymns on Paradise,* trans. S. Brock (Crestwood: St. Vladimir Seminary Press, 1990), 48.

Sin and Death

Working backwards then, let us consider and examine the products and tangible 'evidence' of the Fall that are all too familiar yet perplexing to all: sin, corruption, and death. Using these as mirrors to reflect unseen realities, we will attempt to see through them a clearer picture of the reality of the place called Eden.

Death is a certainty in this world and indeed a great mystery. All creation is filled with life and beauty, and yet strangely everything eventually falls into decay and death. It happens sometimes so slowly that it seems somehow like a 'natural' process; just because seemingly 'that is the way things are'. Why is this so? It is clear that at a personal level man has the power of life and death in his free choice. By choosing what is good and in accordance with the teachings of Christ, one gains peace and life. Conversely, by choosing that which goes against the commandments of God, one brings anguish, destruction, and death upon oneself and one's surroundings.

Adam's greatest sin was that he chose to live a life without God—a life apart from the source of life—which meant death and disintegration. In the biblical-patristic tradition, death is unnatural and seen as an enemy that must be conquered.[7]

---

[7] Many ancient philosophies underpin Western society's vision of death, and inadvertently influence or prejudice our understanding concerning it, seeking to shroud the mystery of death in a false and superficial intellectual security; that somehow everyone that dies goes 'to a better place', and concurrently the body is not a necessary part of human existence, both of which ideas are untrue from an Orthodox Christian perspective. We see the fruition of this idea in modern times with euthanasia and cremation. Everything in modern society is given to busy and entertain people to death, so that they might avoid facing and preparing for the reality of death during

"The last enemy that shall be destroyed is death" (1 Cor. 15:26). For it is written in the Scriptures, "For God made not death: neither does he take pleasure in the destruction of the living. For He created all things, that they might have their being" (Wisd. of Sol. 1:13-14). Man, by his own free choice, brings the possibility of death into this world, because:

> God in the beginning, when He created man, created him holy, passionless and sinless, in His own image and likeness. And man was then precisely like God who created him; for the holy, sinless and passionless God creates also His creatures holy, passionless and sinless. But inasmuch as unalterability and invariability are characteristic of the Unoriginate and Uncreated Divinity alone, therefore the created man naturally was alterable and changeable… there was given to him a commandment not to eat from one tree only, so that he might know that he was alterable and changeable….[8]

Death then is the result of the first-created man's free will. By disobeying the commandments of God and being separated from Life, the first man was allowed to die by the mercy of God so that he would not remain forever separated

---

life. The corruptibility of this world is hidden beneath medicines, baths, cosmetics, and cleaning supplies. Even mortuary homes are pleasant and those who have passed are made to look their best.

[8] St. Symeon the New Theologian, *The Sin of Adam,* Homily 2; quoted in Johanna Manley, *The Lament of Eve* (Menlo Park: Monastery Book, 1993), 723-24.

from Life in "a living death."[9] Death is separation from God, a separation which occurs from sin. Therefore, at the heart of death is sin, "for the wages of sin is death" (Rom. 6:23). Even though through the breaking of God's commandment Adam's soul 'died' and was separated from life, his body was allowed by God's mercy to live for another 930 years, granting time for repentance, so that he might not perish forever. Because Adam and Eve had fallen into corruption, so too the children they produced inherited a similar nature infected with decay and death.

St. Maximus explains that

> After the fall the generation of every man was by nature impassioned and preceded by pleasure. From this rule no one was exempt. On the contrary, as if discharging a natural debt, all underwent sufferings and the death that comes from them…. Man's life originates in the corruption that comes from his generation through pleasure and ends in the corruption that comes through death….[10]

St. Maximus, St. Gregory of Nyssa, St. John Chrysostom, St. Athanasius, and others all teach that God had planned a non-sexual way for the first-created man to procreate in paradisaic conditions.[11] Yet Adam's transgression consequently

---

[9] See St. Basil's homily: *God is not the Cause of Evils* in *On the human condition.*

[10] St. Maximus, *Fourth Century of Various Texts* 39, quoted in *The Philokalia,* vol. 2, 245.

[11] "It should be noted that certain Fathers regard sexual relations (even in the context of marriage) as a consequence of the fall (see e.g. St. Athanasius

made for a different way of procreation, a way that was entangled in corruption and decay,

> [For] when our forefather Adam broke the divine commandment, in the place of the original form of generation he conceived and introduced into human nature, at the prompting of the serpent, another form, originating in pleasure and terminating through suffering in death. This pleasure was not the consequence of antecedent suffering but, rather, resulted in suffering. And because he introduced this ill-gotten pleasure-provoked form of generation, he deservedly brought on himself, and on all men born in the flesh from him, the doom of death through suffering.[12]

The vast consensus of the patristic writings tell us that human nature inherited mortality and corruption as a consequence of Adam's sin, but it does not receive Adam's guilt for his personal transgression (as the Western theologians erroneously teach).[13] Each person is responsible for their own sins,

---

the Great, *Interpretation on the Psalms,* L, 7; and St. John Chrysostom, *On Genesis,* Hom. XV, 4.) In fact it was Adam's fall, which resulted in man's becoming subject to death, that made marriage necessary. For this reason, marriage is recognized as conformity to the post-lapsarian state brought about by death (see St. John Damascene, *On the Orthodox Faith* IV, 24); and St. John Chrysostom claims that if man had not transgressed, God would have multiplied the human race in a different way; the same view being held by St. Maximus the Confessor, in his *Ambigua* XLI (PG 91:1309A)..." (Christopher Veniamin, *St. Gregory of Palamas: The Homilies* [Waymart: Mount Thabor Publishing, 2009], 557).

[12] St. Maximus, *Fourth Century on Various Texts* 44, quoted in *Philokalia,* vol. 2, 246-247.

[13] The teaching of Original Sin (that all are guilty of Adam's sin) was

yet due to the inheritance of death, human nature has been weakened with a deep-seated inclination towards sin and passion, originating from its mortality, creating a vicious cycle of pleasure and pain.

Unfortunately, a faulty interpretation by Western theologians concerning the consequences of Adam's sin had extremely vast ramifications pertaining to the perceptions of how man is saved and what salvation is. One might dare say that how one views Adam is how one will see Christ and His redemptive work. In fact, in the West the concept of justification is dependent on the doctrine of Original Sin.[14] The Eastern and Western ideas concerning salvation and justification consequently are very different.

The biblical-patristic consensus thus far tells us that Adam was undoubtedly ontologically a real man,[15] first-created

---

propagated by Blessed Augustine due to a faulty translation in the Vulgate of St. Paul's Epistle to the Romans. "In the Latin translation of the original Greek text, one important word, *o thanatos* (death) has been omitted from one of the subordinate clauses, and the phrase *eph o*, meaning 'on account of which' or 'because' had been mistranslated as *'in quo'*, meaning 'in whom' or 'in which'. The relative pronoun *quo* could be understood either as masculine referring to Adam, or as neuter referring to sin. In either case, the Latin text of Romans 5:12 seemed to say quite clearly that all had sinned in Adam, or in Adam's sin = 'inherited culpability' that is, the idea that each human individual, from the moment of conception, has inherited the responsibility and guilt for the first sin of Adam as if it were their own" (Weaver, "The Exegesis of Romans 5:12").

[14] "In its second session, the Council of Trent was compelled to define the nature of Original Sin as the indispensable preliminary to the definition of justification, because the whole doctrine of justification is dependent upon the definition of Original Sin" (Weaver, "The Exegesis of Romans 5:12," 203. See also, *Decrees of the Ecumenical Councils,* Council of Trent, Session 5:2-5, 666).

[15] That Adam was a real man doesn't come into question until the 1700's.

between incorruption and corruption in a place beyond all human comprehension, dwelling and abiding in communion with God. Through his disobedience to God's commandment by his free will, he was separated from the source of life, dying first in soul and then in body. From this first man, we inherit death, corrupting our will and inclining us to sin. The Second Adam, the Lord Jesus Christ, appeared some seventy-five generations later at the "fullness of time" (Gal. 4:4); He "abolished death and has brought life and immortality to light through the gospel" (II Tim. 1:10).

The Tree and Paradise

Created between corruption and incorruption,[16] St. Gregory the Sinaite says that

> [Paradise] is always rich in fruits, ripe and unripe, and continually full of flowers. When trees and ripe fruit rot and fall to the ground they turn into sweet-scented soil, free from the smell of decay … because of the great richness and holiness of the grace ever abounding there.[17]

St. John of Damascus says that

---

[16] "Some have imagined Paradise to have been material, while others have imagined it to have been spiritual. However, it seems to me that just as man was created both sensitive [material] and intellectual [spiritual], so did this most sacred domain of his have the twofold aspect of being perceptible both to the senses and to the mind" (St. John of Damascus, "Exposition of the Orthodox Faith," 2:11, quoted from *Nicene and Post Nicene Fathers,* vol. 9, 29).

[17] St. Gregory the Sinaite, *Philokalia,* vol. 4, 213.

> [Paradise] is temperate and the air that surrounds
> it is the rarest and the purest: evergreen plants are
> its pride, sweet fragrances abound, it is flooded
> with light, and in sensuous freshness and beauty
> it transcends imagination…[18]

St. John continues, saying the Tree of the Knowledge of Good
and Evil was planted in the midst of Paradise

> for trial, and proof, and exercise of man's obedi-
> ence and disobedience: and hence it was named
> the Tree of the Knowledge of Good and Evil … to
> those who partook of it was given power to know
> their own nature.[19]

This tree provided a boundary beyond which Adam and Eve
could not go,[20] acting like the curtain in the Old Testament
Tabernacle that separated the holy place from the Holy of
Holies,[21] where the Tree of Life was. Correspondingly, the Tabernacle of the Old Testament and the Church building today
are patterns of this heavenly tabernacle not "made with hands"
(Heb. 9:24).

   The patristic consensus tells us that, before the Fall, Adam
in his natural state had a heart illumined by the All-holy Spirit.[22] Adam's partaking of the Tree disrupted the natural balance
of perception, and his reasoning capacity became the primary
faculty of perception. This caused a usurping of the primary

---

[18] St. John of Damascus, *Exposition*, 2:11, 29-30.

[19] Ibid, 29-30.

[20] St. Ephraim, *Hymns on Paradise*, Hymn III.3.

[21] Ibid., III.5.

[22] See Vlachos, "Catechism of the Orthodox Church," from *Divine Ascent*, Vol. 6.

faculty of the heart, resulting in confusion and a darkening of perception.[23] The Tree was "good if consumed at the proper time, for the tree was *theoria* [the vision of God] which is safe only for those with perfect inclination."[24] Thus, the Tree would have become Adam's deification if partaken of at the proper time.

As Adam partook of the Tree in Paradise, we too are faced with the Tree of the Knowledge of Good and Evil, which St. Maximus says is the world itself.[25] Similarly, the world can lead us to God when it is used properly, serving as a window to see God's infinite mercy and majesty, "for the Heavens are telling of the glory of God and the firmament proclaims His handiwork" (Ps. 18:1 LXX). But conversely, when used apart from God and selfishly for its own sake, it leads to emptiness, death, and hell.

For as in Adam all die, even so in Christ shall all be made alive (1 Cor. 15:22)

The Troparion for the Pre-feast of the Nativity gives a clear picture of the restoration that Christ came to grant to Adam by becoming flesh:

> Make ready, O Bethlehem; open unto all, O Eden. Adorn Thyself, O Ephratha, for the Tree of Life has blossomed forth from the Virgin in the cave. Her womb is shown to be a spiritual Paradise with the Divine Fruit, and those who eat of

---

[23] Ibid., p. 148.
[24] Oration 45, 8, *Nicene and Post-Nicene Fathers*, vol. 2:7:83.
[25] See St. Maximus, *Philokalia*, vol. 2, 175-176.

it will live forever and not die like Adam. Christ
comes to restore the image which He made in the
beginning.[26]

God gave the promise of redemption as He cursed the serpent in the Garden immediately after Adam's transgression:
"I will put enmity between you and the woman, and between
your seed and her seed. He shall bruise your head, and you
shall bruise his heel" (Gen. 3:15). Christ, Who was born of a
woman under the law, came to crush the head of the serpent
by "destroy[ing] him who had the power of death, that is, the
devil" (Heb. 2:14).

The sacraments of the Orthodox Church are not directed
at appeasing or propitiating God and His justice; rather, they
are used to restore communion with the One Who is Life by
conquering death and its inseparable offspring, sin.[27] Christ
destroys what St. Nicholas Cabasilas calls "the triple barrier"[28]
of separation from God: by His Incarnation, He destroys the
separation in nature; by His death on the Cross, He destroys

---

[26] *December Menaion*, Prefeast of the Nativity of Christ (Liberty: St.
John of Kronstadt Press), 1996.

[27] "For we believe that at birth a person has a pure nous: his nous is
illuminated, which is the natural state. The inheritance of ancestral sin, as
we said in another place, lies in the fact that the body inherits corruptibility
and mortality, which, with the passage of time, and as [a] the child grows
and passions develop, darkens the noetic part of his soul.... By holy Baptism
we are not getting rid of guilt from ancestral sin, but we are being grafted
onto the body of Christ, the Church, and are acquiring the power to conquer
death" (Vlachos, *Life After Death*, 101).

[28] St. Nicholas Cabasilas, *The Life in Christ* (Crestwood: St. Vladimir
Press, 1974), 106.

the separation by sin; and by His Resurrection, He destroys the separation of death.[29]

Christ was born of the Virgin to have a nature like Adam's before the Fall.[30] As Eve was taken from the rib of Adam and Adam from the virginal ground, so too Christ was taken from the virgin earth of the Theotokos, that He might not be infected with the *passiblity* (corruption) and *peccability* (tendency to sin) that is inherited by the mode of engendering to which mankind became subject. The virgin birth of Christ is the indispensable hub which the plan of God's salvation revolves around, making a new way for spiritual regeneration from above through His generation, being born of the Virgin that we might be born in the Spirit.

St. Maximus tells us that Christ's "nature was without sin because His birth in time from a woman was not preceded by the slightest trace of that pleasure arising from the primal disobedience."[31] Thus, the True God and Creator of Adam took on all of Adam—his corruption and death—yet by not being engendered by a carnal conception, Christ avoided the instability of a corruptible will which tended towards disintegration and sin. Hence, Christ had an immutability in the disposition of His will which contributed to delivering human nature from the bondage of corruption and its effects on the will. He came to set our free choice aright because

---

[29] Vladimir Lossky, *The Mystical Theology of the Eastern Church* (Crestwood: St. Vladimir Press, 1976), 136.

[30] Georges Florovsky, *Byzantine Fathers of the Sixth to Eighth Century,* trans. Raymond Miller (Vaduz: Buchervertriebsanstalt, 1987), 290.

[31] St. Maximus, *Philokalia*, vol. 2, 245.

> Adam, [in] turning his disposition of will and his choice towards evil, had introduced passibility, corruption … [yet] Christ through the immutability of his disposition of will and choice, frees it from sin and restores to it, through resurrection, impassibility, incorruption, and immortality.…[32]

Hence, Christ works to reverse all that was done by the first-created man. By His Passion He conferred on us dispassion and by His death He brought us eternal life. His selfless obedience on the Cross and the incorruptibility of His will during pain, temptation, and death correspondingly healed the selfish disobedience of Adam which brought the corruption of the human will, one which came from the seeking of pleasure:

> Pleasure and pain were not created simultaneously with the flesh. On the contrary, it was the fall that led man to conceive and pursue pleasure in a way that corrupted his power of choice, and that also brought upon him, by way of chastisement, the pain that leads to the dissolution of his nature.[33]

The Gospel's great truth is that there is salvation and healing for all people: the Cross! This is why Christ's words to those who follow Him prove so true and powerfully transformative: "Deny [yourself], take up [your] Cross, and follow Me" (Matt. 16:24). St. Ignatius Brianchaninov explains that there is a wonderful relationship between the Cross and the commandments

---

[32] Jean Claude Larchet, *Sobornost*, 20:1, (1998), 40.
[33] St. Maximus, *Philokalia*, vol. 2, 244.

of Christ: when one chooses to do the commandments, the Cross is placed on our backs to carry, revealing a fallen state of the will that rebels against God which man must struggle against.[34] The beginning of the way back to Paradise for "the old man" (Eph. 4:22) is to suffer and die with Christ; that "the new man" (Eph. 4:24) might find the Resurrection through being joined to the corporate Body of Christ, "impelling the whole of nature to rise like dough in the Resurrection of Life."[35]

Following the commandments, when empowered by the Spirit through the sacramental life, putting to death the corruptible will which causes the disintegration of our whole person through sin and unnatural passions; when the new man arises through baptism, empowered by the Spirit to perform virtue, he dwells in Christ by keeping the commandments, uniting himself through virtue to goodness, which is God's energies.[36] Therefore, the one who sees God through the purification of the heart is the one who "is crucified … to the world" (Gal. 6:14) by keeping the commandments, "always bearing about in the body the dying of the Lord Jesus, that the life of Jesus also might be made manifest in our body" (II Cor. 4:10).

As previously stated, St. John Chrysostom tells us that Christ came to set aright our free choice for

---

[34] See Ignatius Brianchaninov, *The Arena* (Jordanville: Holy Trinity Monastery, 1983).

[35] See St. Maximus, "On the Lord's Prayer," *Philokalia,* vol. 4.

[36] "Some things began to be in time, for they have not always existed. Others did not begin to be in time, for goodness, blessedness, holiness and immortality have always existed. Those things which began in time exist and are said to exist by participation in the things which did not begin in time" (St. Maximus, *Philokalia*, vol. 2, 150).

> the fall was a volitional act, and therefore an
> injury to human will, a disconnecting of human
> will and God's will … [therefore] healing must
> be the doctoring and restoration of the human
> will….[37]

From holy baptism and chrismation onward, Christians are no longer under the dominion of sin, "for [they] are not under the Law, but under grace … for the Law of the Spirit of Life in Christ Jesus has made [them] free from the Law of sin and death" (Rom. 6:14, 8:3). Why? Because our "old man is crucified with Him, that the body of sin might be destroyed, that henceforth we should not serve sin" (Rom. 6:6). By becoming united to Christ, one body with Him through the sacramental life, we become part of His very "flesh and … bones" (Eph. 5:30), and subsequently we participate in His victory over sin and death. The holiness of the saints is due to the fact that they have united their will to the will of Christ.[38]

Christ's saving dispensation was of an absolute ontological necessity, for we know that "what is not assumed is not healed."[39] Everything that was lying in a state of corruption had to be restored by the incorruptible Word Who became flesh. It wasn't renewed by a wave of God's hand, but in an actual concrete action:

---

[37] Quoted from Florovsky, *Byzantine Fathers of the Sixth to Eighth Century*, 230.

[38] St. Nicholas Cabasilas, *PG* 613, quoted in Nellas, *Redemption or Deification*.

[39] St. Gregory the Theologian, *Epistle to Cledonius*, in *Nicene and Post-Nicene Fathers*, vol. 7.

> Forasmuch then as the children are partakers of flesh and blood, He also Himself likewise took part of the same, that through death He might destroy him that had the power of death, that is the devil: and deliver them who through fear of death were all their lifetime subject to bondage. For verily He took not on Himself the nature of angels; but He took on Himself the seed of Abraham (Heb. 2:14-16).

We can see Adam in ourselves primarily through our mortality, corruptibility, and our fallenness. Some modern Christian writers have said it is uncertain which might be a worse state: not to believe in God, or not to believe in one's own fallenness. To become like Christ, the Second Adam, we must realize and see in ourselves the image and the marks of the first Adam, for the two are inseparably linked. It is only when we are deeply aware of the death in ourselves that we have the opportunity to know and see Christ as He truly is: the Life and Savior of all.

Thus, the importance of the ascetic struggle in this world must be an Orthodox Christian's primary concern, not for the sake of placating God, but for healing our hearts, being purified of the passions and sins that bring death. Christianity without the Cross of the ascetic life is utopianism. To re-enter Paradise, one must follow Christ to the Cross, personally experiencing the suffering and death of the old man which, though momentary, leads us to an exceeding and "eternal weight of glory" (11 Cor. 4:17). Adam, in his refusal to fast and in his search for pleasure, brought about his expulsion from

Paradise, while Christ's sufferings[40] and death brought about healing and eternal life. Therefore we too must willingly and thankfully endure the sufferings of the flesh and disdain its pleasures; for the first restores God's blessings while the second separates us from those blessings.[41]

The Cross of Christ is the true Tree of Life, which is Christ Himself. Seen from this side of Paradise, in a post-lapsarian state, the Cross looks like an instrument of death, humiliation and "foolishness" (1 Cor. 1:18). Yet when seen from the side of Paradise it is the Tree of incorruption, of an unfathomably luminous glory, and the very symbol "of the Son of the Living One."[42] St. Ephraim even says, "Greatly saddened was the Tree of Life when it beheld Adam stolen away from it; it sank down into the virgin ground and was hidden—to burst forth and reappear on Golgotha...."[43]

By eating the fruit of the Tree of the Cross, the Eucharist, we gain that Life of immortality and deification which Adam was supposed to attain. Through the Cross, "the perfect redemption of fallen Adam," Christ "raised us up, who were exiles far from God, whom the enemy despoiled of old through pleasure...."[44]

---

[40] "And if because of the tree of food they were then cast out of Paradise, shall not believers now more easily enter into Paradise because of the tree of Jesus?" (St. Cyril of Jerusalem, *Nicene and Post-Nicene Fathers,* vol. 7).

[41] St. Maximus, *Philokalia,* vol. 2, 170.

[42] St. Ephraim, *Hymns on Paradise,* 16.

[43] Ibid., 60.

[44] *Lenten Triodion,* Matins: Veneration of the Cross, 3rd Sunday of Lent, 348-49.

The Church "has been revealed as a second Paradise, having within it, like the first Paradise of old, a Tree of Life, the Cross of the Lord."[45] Therefore the Church triumphantly sings:

> Come, Adam and Eve, our first father and mother, who fell from the choir on high through the envy of the murderer of man, when of old with bitter pleasure ye tasted from the tree in Paradise. See, the Tree of the Cross, revered by all, draws near! Run with haste and embrace it joyfully, and cry to it with faith: O precious Cross, thou art our succour; partaking of thy fruit, we have gained incorruption; we are restored once more to Eden, and we have received great mercy.[46]

The Person of Christ reunites in Himself heaven and earth; for wherever Christ is, it is Paradise. Nothing hinders communion with God now except for our unbelief and free choice. And yet Paradise cannot necessarily be seen as a locality from our current point of view, for we know that "the kingdom of God is within" (Luke 17:21). As St. Maximus explains,

> [the] inheritance of the saints is God Himself, [and] he who is found worthy of this grace will be beyond all ages, times and places: he will have God Himself as his place.[47]

The whole world is drawn back into Paradise through our union with Christ.

---

[45] Ibid., Matins: Veneration of the Cross, 3rd Sunday of Lent, 341.

[46] Ibid., Vespers: Lord I call, 3rd Sunday of Lent, 335.

[47] St. Maximus, *Philokalia*, vol. 2, 168.

Adam received the curse: "Cursed is the ground for your sake ... thorns also and thistles shall it bring forth" (Gen. 3:16-17); for this cause, Christ received the crown of thorns. Adam realized he was naked and was expelled from the garden; Christ hung naked on the Cross, bringing us back into Paradise. The sword was placed to guard the Tree of Life; the sword that pierced Christ's side removed it. Adam stretched out his hands in disobedience; Christ stretched out His hands in obedience to the Father. Adam ate of the forbidden Tree out of pride, wanting to become like God; Christ tasted gall and bitterness in humiliation and the unthinkable self-emptying of His divinity (Phil. 2:5-8). As St. Paul says, "For since by man came death, by man came also the resurrection of the dead. For as all in Adam die, even so in Christ shall all be made alive" (1 Cor. 15:21-22).

In short, Adam failed to fulfill his calling; but Christ, point-by-point, set aright the stumblings of the first-created man. God foreknew Adam would fail; nevertheless, the Incarnation would have taken place, for Christ is the Lamb of God who "was foreordained before the foundation of the world" (1 Pet. 1:20). The Lamb would not only take away the sins of the world and destroy death, but also fulfill the "mystery from eternity" (Col. 1:26): that at the "fullness of time" (Eph. 1:10), God would recapitulate all of creation in Christ.

For St. Maximus, the Incarnation is the primary reason for the creation of man—so that God might "be all in all" (1 Cor. 15:28). God

> had an ineffably good plan for created beings long before the ages and before those beings. The plan was for Him to mingle, without change on

His part, with human nature by true hypostatic
union [i.e., union in His person], to unite human
nature to Himself while remaining immutable, so
that he might become a man, as He alone knew
how, and might make humanity divine in union
with Himself.[48]

At the very heart of the reason for creation is the Incarnation; and subsequently, the deification of all of creation. This
is the Gospel: that the old Adam was created for the Second
Adam! For

it was for the new man [i.e., Christ] that human
nature was created in the beginning ... for it was
not the old Adam who was the model for the new,
but the new Adam for the old.[49]

Adam was made in the image of God (Gen. 1:26) and Christ is
that image of God (Col. 1:15, II Cor. 4:4).

Therefore, our worldview must radically shift. Christ is not
only the Savior, but the Alpha and the Omega; He is the archetype towards which every created thing tends, for all things
"were created by Him and for Him" (Col 1:16), to be united
with Him. It was Adam who was formed in the beginning to
be able to receive God so that he might be a partaker "of the
divine nature" (II Pet. 1:4). Christ, trampling down death by

---

[48] *Questions to Thalassios*, 55 quoted from Paul Blowers, *Exegesis and
Spiritual Pedagogy in Maximus the Confessor* (Notre Dame: University of
Notre Dame, 1991), 129.

[49] St. Nicholas Cabasilas, *PG* 680A, quoted in Nellas, *Redemption or Deification*, 16.

death, brought Adam back to life, and by virtue of His Incarnation made Adam a partaker of the Life of God.

We can thus conclude that Adam, the first man, being created in a way that is beyond our understanding, through his disobedience infected human nature with corruption, sin, and death. Christ, the Second Adam, came, and through the Tree of the Cross conquered that death coming from the first Tree. By destroying death, He destroyed death's inseparable companion: sin. Consequently, when we are united in the sacramental life to the Church, the real and living Body of Christ, we are freed from the power of sin and death. By grace, our will is empowered to fulfill the commandments, restoring the image of God in us, bringing about His likeness in us.

Thus the whole creation begins the movement to attain to its end. Through the dynamic transforming action of the Church, the uncreated and the created are joined in an inseparable marriage, without confusion, division, or change, through and in the Body of Christ. Thus begins the restoration of Paradise in this world which awaits the end of this process after the Second Coming of our Lord Jesus Christ.[50]

---

[50] Also see Rom. 8:20-23; Isa. 65:17; Rev. 21.

St. Augustine and Orthodoxy: In Light of the Eastern Church Fathers

THE PLACE OF ST. AUGUSTINE OF HIPPO in the Orthodox Church is often an issue of contention in our day. It has been said that no other Christian writer, within the East or the West, has had more historical influence than has the North African Bishop of Hippo.[1] Although the authenticity of his Christian witness has been affirmed and substantiated by many Church Fathers,[2] as Orthodox believers it is nonetheless imperative (especially in our post-modern Western society) to reverently approach St. Augustine's theological teachings with great caution.

---

[1] See J. Pelikan, *The Emergence of Catholic Tradition*, vol. 1 (Chicago: University of Chicago Press, 1971), 292.

[2] E.g., St. Mark of Ephesus used Augustine's writings extensively against the Latins at the Council of Florence, referring to him as the 'divine Augustine.' St. Dimitri of Rostov, in the 18th century, also entered St. Augustine's veneration in his Great Menology. However, this angered many Russian theologians since they saw it as an endorsement of Scholastic theology. See *The Synaxarion*, June 15, vol. 5, trans. Mother Maria (Ormylia: Holy Convent of the Annunciation of Our Lady, 2008), 515.

St. Photius the Great writes about St. Augustine,

> Knowing that some of the Fathers and Doctors
> have deviated from the Faith in certain dogmas,
> we do not receive as doctrine those matters in
> which they have deviated, but we no less con-
> tinue to extend the hand of friendship to those
> men.[3]

Father Makarios of Simonas Petras Monastery on Mount
Athos comments, in his *Synaxarion* for June 15, on the problematic nature of some aspects of St. Augustine's teachings:

> Urged both by his intellectual formation and the
> circumstances of his conversion to envisage the
> relationship of man with God from a more or less
> 'psychological' point of view, differing from that
> adopted by earlier patristic tradition, St. Augus-
> tine gave all his theology a personal aspect, which
> influenced his doctrine of the Holy Trinity, Origi-
> nal Sin, the relationship between nature and grace,
> etc. As long as these theses were considered to be
> personal theological opinions (*theologoumena*),
> they were no impediment to the veneration of
> Augustine in the ranks of Orthodox saints. It was
> only when they were adopted as the official and
> exclusive doctrine of the Roman Church (notably
> the *Filioque*), that they became the main subject
> of dissension…. If one can rightly venerate St.
> Augustine as an Orthodox saint, it is less for his

---

[3] St. Photius the Great, *Epistle* 24. 20, quoted from *The Synaxarion*, ibid.

qualities as a theologian than as a pastor, and for
his undeniable personal sanctity.... It is enough
here to make this distinction between his life and
the unfortunate development of his doctrine.[4]

This chapter discusses certain elements in St. Augustine's thought that are problematic in light of Orthodox patristic teaching. Although his genius is indisputable, the manner in which some of his theological teachings are interpreted and applied are often a cause of great concern. Through this brief presentation, it is hoped that the reader will gain a better appreciation for the precision of Orthodox theological thought and the dangers that subtle divergences can produce.

A Brief Biographical Overview

St. Augustine was born in Numidia (modern Algeria) in Northern Africa on November 13, 354 of a pagan father and a Christian mother, St. Monica (commemorated on May 4). Although he was raised with a Christian education, he began to lead a sinful life in his mid-teens and fostered a child out of wedlock when he was seventeen. While teaching rhetoric in Carthage at the age of nineteen in 373, he joined the dualistic sect of the Manicheans.

After nine years, in 382, Augustine became disillusioned and left the sect, moving to Rome where he began a school for oratory. Augustine eventually applied for a professorship in Milan in 384 where he providentially heard a series of sermons on the truth of the Holy Scriptures given by the

---

[4] *The Synaxarion*, ibid.

ruling Bishop of Milan, St. Ambrose. Inspired and challenged, Augustine was baptized three years later by St. Ambrose on Holy Saturday in the year 387. Soon after returning to Africa in 388, Augustine was ordained priest in 391, and eventually consecrated bishop in 395.

Throughout his episcopacy, St. Augustine was faced with several problems plaguing the Church in Carthage, among the most significant, Donatism and Pelagianism. These conflicts which dealt with the nature of man, grace, and salvation deeply influenced the content and tone of his writings. St. Augustine reposed on August 28, 430 at the age of seventy-five.

Augustine's Theological Method: The Influence of Neoplatonism

Henry Chadwick referred to St. Augustine as the first "modern man" due to his "extraordinary psychological depth."[5] Augustine is also referred to as "the Christian Plato."[6] It was stated by the Jesuit Augustinian scholar Eugene Portalie, that in the early years after his conversion, Augustine was basically still "a neoplatonist[7] who had become a very sincere Christian … still trying to couch the dogmas of his faith in neoplatonic expressions."[8]

---

[5] Henry Chadwick, *Augustine* (New York: Oxford University Press, 1986), 3.

[6] See A. H. Armstrong, *Introduction to Ancient Philosophy* (London: Methuen), 205.

[7] Neoplatonism, originating in the 3rd century AD, was a mixture of platonism and Eastern mysticism. Among other doctrines, it teaches that the soul is preexistent and divine in origin.

[8] Eugene Portalie, *A Guide to the Thought of Saint Augustine,* trans. R. Bastian (Chicago: Henry Regnery), 96.

Augustine himself noted that because his knowledge of Greek was so poor, he read very few books of Plato[9] and had to rely on Latin translations. He was heavily influenced by Victorinus' translations of the neoplatonist philosophers Plotinus and Porphyry, which he speaks about at length.[10]

The influence of neoplatonism on St. Augustine's thought is uncontested.[11] For this reason, his 'theological' method is often more 'philosophical,' especially when compared with the traditional theological approach of the Eastern Church Fathers. The Orthodox approach to theology is based on a life dedicated to the pursuit of prayer through personal participation in the ascetic, sacramental, and liturgical life of the Church. It is not based on discursive reasoning.

It might be said that one of the foremost difficulties with Augustine's thought is that he maintained a neoplatonist approach to understanding both God and human nature, which is based thoroughly on man's reasoning and rational abilities.[12] This is what essentially separates Augustine from the Eastern Orthodox theological tradition. His approach is based more on philosophical concepts rather than on the experiential methodology inherited from the Church Fathers before him.

---

[9] E.g., see Augustine, *On the Blessed Life*, 1. 4.

[10] See Augustine, *The Confessions*, 8. 2, and *The City of God,* 7 and 8.

[11] Augustine compared the writings of Plotinus with Holy Scripture, "In my desire to apprehend truth not only by faith but also by understanding—I feel sure at the moment that I shall find it with the Platonists, nor will it be at variance with our sacred mysteries" (*Against the Academics*, 3. 20, 43, trans. J. O'Meara [New York: Newman, 1951], 150).

[12] See *Augustine Through the Ages*, ed. A. Fitzgerald (Grand Rapids, Eerdman's, 1999), 699. See also, *Confessions*, 7. 1 and *City of God*, 8. 5.

Even a brief reading shows how Augustine's theological method is at times inconsistent with traditional Orthodox experience. Augustine clearly remains embedded within a neoplatonic framework.[13] He fails to make a clear distinction between the human mind and what can be perceived beyond the created mind's thoughts and capacities.[14] The neoplatonic model considers the human mind as capable of knowing or understanding God, due to the platonic presupposition that the soul itself is divine, and thus merely on a quest to find its 'deeper self'. This idea concerning the soul's divinity was of necessity rejected by Augustine, yet he readily retained the first premise pertaining to his inflated regard for man's rational and intellectual ability to know God.

St. Maximus the Confessor explains a critical patristic distinction that St. Augustine fails to consider:

---

[13] "Plotinus ... inherits to the full that self-confident Hellenistic theological rationalism, that belief that a human philosopher can by his own powers give a satisfactory account of divine things, which has its roots in the conviction that man himself is by nature divine" (Armstrong, *An Introduction to Ancient Philosophy,* 179).

[14] Augustine writes, "The human soul is never anything but reasonable or intellectual; and therefore ... made according to the image of God ... it is able to use its reason and intelligence to understand and to behold God..." (*On the Trinity* 14. 4 [6], trans. S. McKenna [Washington DC: Catholic University of America Press, 1963], 418). He writes elsewhere, "Let them consider this well and weigh these words, who believe that the beginning of faith is of our doing and that only the supplementing of faith is from God. For who would not see that thinking comes before believing? For no one believes anything, unless he has first thought that it is to be believed.... still it is necessary that all things which are believed, are believed after thought has preceded" (*On the Predestination of the Saints* 5, trans. Mourant and Collinge [Washington DC: Catholic University of America Press, 1992], 221-22).

The intelligence recognizes two kinds of knowledge of divine realities. The first is relative, because it is confined to the intelligence and its intellections [i.e., thoughts], and does not entail any real perception, through actual experience, of what is known. The second is true and authentic knowledge. Through experience alone and through grace it brings about, by means of participation and *without the help of the intelligence and its intellections,* a total and active perception of what is known. It is through this second kind of knowledge that, when we come into our inheritance [i.e., eternal salvation], we receive supra-natural and ever-activated deification.... This real knowledge, which through experience and participation brings about a perception of what is known, supersedes the knowledge that resides in the intelligence and the intellections.... The second consists solely in the actual enjoyment of divine realities through direct vision....[15]

For the Orthodox Church, man's created reason can never apprehend the uncreated things of God, for they are radically dissimilar. As St. Maximus explains elsewhere, we must *transcend* ourselves and our mind's activity and all else that belongs to this world if we are to receive "a ray of divine knowledge."[16]

---

[15] St. Maximus, *Various Texts,* 29, quoted from *Philokalia,* vol. 2, 242.

[16] "Our [nous] possesses ... the capacity for a union that transcends its nature and that unites it with what is beyond its natural scope. It is through this union that divine realities are apprehended, not by means of our own natural capacities, but by virtue of the fact that we entirely transcend ourselves.... This [the nous] does by transcending all that belongs to the sensible

St. Dionysius the Areopagite discusses the depth of divine transcendence:

> When we say anything about God, we should set down the truth "not in the plausible words of human wisdom but in demonstration of the power granted by the Spirit" to the scripture writers, a power by which, in a manner surpassing speech and knowledge, we reach a union superior to anything available to us by way of our own abilities or activities in the realm of discourse or of intellect. This is why we must not dare to resort to words or conceptions concerning that hidden divinity which transcends being, apart from what the sacred scriptures have divinely revealed.[17]

In this light, we must conclude that the things of God are not known by the rational mind alone, but rather they are experienced in the heart of man. This is attained only in Christ, through the life in Christ as living members of His holy Body, the Church.

Fr. John Romanides explains the primary problem in Augustine's approach,

> For Augustine, there is no distinction between revelation [which is directly from God] and conceptual intuition of revelation [which is thinking

---

[material] and intelligible [spiritual] worlds, and even its own activity; for only thus may it receive the ray of divine knowledge" (St. Maximus, *Various Texts*, 5. 68, 69, Ibid., 276).

[17] St. Dionysius the Areopagite, *The Divine Names* 1. 1, trans. C. Luibheld (New York: Paulist Press, 1987), 49.

about God]. Whether revelation is given directly
to human reason, or to human reason by means
of creatures [i.e., angels] or created symbols, [for
Augustine] it is always the human intellect [i.e.,
rational mind] itself which is being illumined or
given vision to.[18]

Within this unique system, Augustine categorically denies
the possibility of the uncreated vision of God—even to the
prophet Moses.[19] This general divergence in theological out-
look proves to be Augustine's point of departure from the
Eastern Orthodox patristic tradition. He clearly explains how
"creatures" (i.e., angels) are used by God to communicate His
"being" to man, whereas the Eastern Orthodox view holds that
it is His own *uncreated* energies through which God commu-
nicates His own uncreated being, life, and glory.

Augustine's theological system thus fails to discern the critical Orthodox distinction between the uncreated *essence* and
the uncreated *energies* of God.[20] The Eastern patristic distinction between the divine essence and energies of God and the
Orthodox experience of man's participation in the uncreated
energies of God remain foreign to him.

In reference to the theophanies[21] of the Old Testament,
Augustine writes that it was an encounter with a created
being or beings that occurred for all those who encountered

[18] J. Romanides, *Franks, Romans, Feudalism, and Doctrine* (Brookline:
Holy Cross Orthodox Press, 1981), 76.

[19] E.g., see *On the Trinity* 2. 16 (27). See also, *A Guide to the Thought*, 111.

[20] The essence of God will always remain unknowable and unpartici-
pable. However, man has the potential to participate in and know God
through His energies.

[21] Theophany, meaning "an appearance of God."

God, whether they be the patriarchs or prophets of the Old Testament:

> It is, therefore, clear that all those things which were shown to the fathers, wherein God made Himself known to them according to His own dispensation, suitable to those times, *came about through a creature*.... When God was said to appear to the fathers of ancient times before the coming of the Savior, those voices and those corporeal forms *were wrought by angels*.[22]

Augustine never came to appreciate the fundamental theological distinction between the revelation of the uncreated glory of the pre-Incarnate *Logos* (i.e., Christ) in the Old Testament and that of the Incarnate *Logos* in the New Testament. Neither did he uphold the basic patristic distinction between the divine and uncreated *essence* and the *energies* of God. Without such crucial theological distinctions, God is limited to revealing Himself only through created means.[23] Consequently, for Augustine, there will always remain an unbridgeable gulf or chasm between the Creator and His creation. Therefore man can never enjoy true communion with God in Christ—which is the very basis of Orthodox spiritual life.

Regardless of his views on divine revelation, and speaking in general terms, one cannot deny the fact of the lingering

---

[22] Augustine, *On the Trinity*, 3. 11 (22, 27), 119, 126 [italics added].

[23] "What did Moses see? Moses saw a cloud, he saw an angel, he saw a fire. All that is the creature: it bore the type of its Lord, but did not manifest the presence of the Lord Himself" (*Tractates on the Gospel of John* 3. 17, from *Nicene and Post Nicene Fathers* vol. 7, trans. J. Gibb [Peabody: Hendrickson, 2004], 23).

influence of unredeemed neoplatonism on Augustine's theological thought. Philosophical baggage seem to separate him from a more Orthodox patristic worldview. This has the potential to lead to a false and fragmented view of spiritual life.[24] This also unfortunately applies to other areas of his theological writings.

Some conclusions drawn from Augustine's philosophical method are not easily understood nor explained. In many places, Augustine seems to be in keeping with the Church's scriptural and patristic tradition. Yet one still finds many inconsistencies and errors in his writings that question the overall integrity of his work and his overall theological vision.[25]

At other times, it is not necessarily what Augustine has *said*, but more often what he has *failed to say*, concisely and clearly, which lends itself to an imprecision and incompleteness in interpreting his voluminous writings. Many have been led into error in their attempt to complete or interpret Augustine's

---

[24] Today, this mindset often manifests itself in a unique way in Western Christianity: the 'either/or' syndrome. Either faith or works, either divine grace or human freedom, either Scripture or Tradition, either Word or Sacrament, *etc.* This mentality may not be entirely disconnected from the many seminal ideas sprinkled throughout Augustine's thought. These completely contrary and opposing views are for the most part unknown in the history of the Orthodox Church, where many of the Western 'either/or' questions are often answered as: 'both/and'.

[25] On certain points in his theology, Augustine changed his mind on key issues, which leaves one uncertain of his doctrinal stability and integrity, especially since on these particular points he veered far away from the Orthodox experience and patristic understanding. In other cases, such as the nature and the generation of the human soul, Augustine puts forth different 'possibilities' and then leaves his reader to choose, commenting that in the end the inquiry "raises more questions than it answers" (*Fathers of the Church Patristic Series: The Retractions*, 2.24.50, trans. Sr. Mary Inez Bogan R.S.M. [Washington DC: The Catholic University of America Press, 1999]).

thought. The Augustinian scholar, Allen Fitzgerald warns of the complexity in approaching the writings of St. Augustine:

> Through the centuries innumerable readers with incommensurable concerns and conflicting perspectives have found much of value in his words, yet these readers have often fundamentally disagreed on what his words meant. Thus, how one understands Augustine depends largely on which of his writings one reads and on the context in which one reads them.[26]

Augustine and the Holy Trinity

Augustine's teaching on the Holy Trinity clearly diverges from that of the Church Fathers of the East. This difference is so marked that the renowned Church historian Jaroslav Pelikan states that when the Orthodox and Augustinian teachings on the Holy Trinity are compared, there are basically two divergent conceptions of God.[27] The differences may seem trivial to some, but in reality they forge the foundation for the Western doctrine of the *Filioque*,[28] which continues to be a major

---

[26] *Augustine Through the Ages,* 716.

[27] Pelikan notes, "Opposed to each other were not only two systems of dogmatic authority and two conceptions of tradition and two methods of formulating theological distinctions, but, beyond and beneath all of these, two conceptions of the Godhead" (Jaroslav Pelikan, *The Christian Tradition, vol. 2: The Spirit of Eastern Christendom* [Chicago: University of Chicago, 1974], 196).

[28] The *filioque,* literally meaning "and the Son," is a later addition to the Nicene-Constantinopolitan Creed. It is the non-Orthodox interpolation of the words "and the Son" after the phrase, "and in the Holy Spirit, the Lord and Giver of Life, who proceeds from the Father...." The Second Ecumenical Council anathematized anyone, or any group, who would ever dare to add

theological factor separating Roman Catholicism from the Orthodox Church.

Augustine's doctrine concerning the Holy Trinity begins by over-emphasizing the unity of the one divine nature of the Trinity (or the one divine 'essence') to the point of undermining the significance of the distinction of the three divine Persons (or the three divine 'hypostases', to use the original Greek term). This clearly presents a platonic priority of unity of 'nature' over distinction of 'person'. It is true that some Augustinian scholars claim this to be an oversimplification. Yet others disagree. Portalie clearly shows how Augustine considered the Holy Trinity primarily as one divine nature—and only then does he proceed to distinguish the three divine Persons.[29]

In contrast, the Eastern Orthodox approach is to first *experience* the divine life of the Holy Trinity and then only later to reflect on the distinction of Persons while at the same time clearly upholding their oneness of nature or essence. For example, St. Gregory the Theologian teaches emphatically,

> No sooner do I conceive of the One than I am illumined by the Splendor of the Three; no sooner do I distinguish Them than I am carried back to the One. When I think of any One of the Three I think of Him as the Whole, and my eyes are filled, and the greater part of what I am thinking of escapes me.[30]

---

to the original Creed.

[29] See Portalie, "In his explanation of the Trinity, Augustine conceives the divine nature before the persons.... foreshadowing the Latin concept which the Scholastics borrowed from him, [Augustine] considered the divine nature before all else..." (*A Guide to the Thought of Augustine*, 130).

[30] St. Gregory of Nazianzos, *Orations* 40. 41, trans. Browne and Swallow

Clearly, St. Gregory the Theologian holds the divine unity and the distinction of the three Persons in a balanced harmony. However, in face of the reaction to the Western emphasis on unity of nature, it is often construed that the Orthodox East prioritizes person over nature, which itself is also a misunderstanding.

Augustine's seemingly simple and harmless neoplatonic method emphasizing unity of nature over distinction of persons has tremendous theological ramifications. It impacts and informs his entire theological teaching. It is obvious that more philosophical, anthropocentric, and even psychological presuppositions are taken for granted. Such an approach remains foreign to the experiential perspective of the Eastern Church Fathers.

Furthermore, from the Orthodox patristic view, theology is a matter of one's personal experience of purification, illumination, and deification in Christ. It is participation in the uncreated glory (or the divine uncreated 'energy' or 'energies') of God. It is this participation which brings true knowledge of God. This participation in the divine glory, light, and life of God constitutes not simply a onetime event for a particular prophet, apostle, or saint, but rather it is an ongoing experience within the life of the Church. This experience of God as 'Person' is the foundation of true theological knowledge: "And this is eternal life, that they may know Thee, the One True God, and Jesus Christ Whom Thou hast sent" (John 17:3).

(Grand Rapids: Eerdmans, 1989), 375. See also St. John Climacus, "… I worship a Trinity in Unity and a Unity in Trinity" (*The Ladder of Divine Ascent*, 221).

It seems that this fundamental difference in Augustine's triadology[31] concerning his over-emphasis on the unity of God's nature (or essence)—which has tremendous theological ramifications—comes from his lack of a clear understanding of 'person' (or 'hypostasis') as defined by the Eastern Church Fathers. Augustine always struggled to conceive of God in terms of 'person'. In fact he was unhappy with the term 'person' and only reluctantly conceded to its usage.[32]

This revolutionary advancement in the patristic concept of 'person' was clearly defined in the triadology of the Cappadocian Fathers (Ss. Basil the Great, Gregory the Theologian, and Gregory of Nyssa). They elucidated the proper balance between the unity of nature and the distinction of the three concrete Persons (or 'hypostases') of the Holy Trinity.[33] St. Basil taught that if we fail or refuse to use the term 'person', we will be in danger of falling into the heresy of Sabellianism.[34]

Augustine, on the other hand, particularly in his work *On the Trinity,* clearly reveals an under-developed grasp and

---

[31] Triadology, meaning "teachings on the Trinity."

[32] E.g., see *On the Trinity* 5. 9 (10).

[33] Since the Cappadocian Fathers wrote in Greek, Augustine was obviously hindered from grasping the full content of their teaching. Cf. *Confessions* 1. 13.

[34] E.g., St. Basil the Great, *Letters* 210. Sabellianism was an ancient Christian heresy also known as 'modalism'. It was a form of monarchianism which, in an attempt to safeguard monotheism, considered the three divine Persons of the Holy Trinity merely as different 'masks' or temporal 'modes' that the One God assumes or puts on at different times. It was an attempt to preserve philosophical monotheism at the expense of the Gospel Truth. It was seen as heretical as it blurred the personal distinctions of the three divine Persons. See G. Florovsky, *Eastern Fathers of the Fourth Century* (Vaduz: Buchervertriebsanstalt, 1987), 96.

true lack of appreciation for the theological term 'hyposta-sis.'[35] He chooses rather to see the Persons more in terms of 'relations' within the one divine essence.[36] Problematically, he over-emphasizes the unity of the one divine essence over and above the distinctions of the three divine Persons, to the point of proclaiming that the Holy Spirit proceeds from *both* the Father and the Son as from one principle. Augustine writes clearly,

> We have to confess that the Father and the Son
> are the principle of the Holy Spirit, not two prin-
> ciples; but as the Father and the Son are one God,
> and in relation to the creature are one Creator
> and one Lord, so they are one principle in rela-
> tion to the Holy Spirit.[37]

Such a teaching attributes to the Son a characteristic which belongs only to the Father. It thus confuses and undermines the unique personal distinctions which distinguish the three divine Persons within the one Holy Trinity.[38] This confusion of personal distinctions would lead later to the full-blown teaching of the *Filioque* which views the Holy Spirit as pro-ceeding from both the Father *and* the Son *as from one*

---

[35] See *On the Trinity,* 5. 8 (9).

[36] E.g., see *On the Trinity* 7. 6 (11). See also J. Kelly, *Early Christian Doc-trines* (New York: Harper and Collins, 1978), 274-275.

[37] *On the Trinity* 5. 14 (15), 193-194. See also *On the Trinity* 15. 26 (46).

[38] The distinguishing marks or properties of the *unbegottenness* of the Father, the *begottenness* of the Son and the *procession* of the Holy Spirit are known as the 'modes of origin' (which is also at times translated as 'way of existence' or 'manner of being'). Each 'mode of origin' is particular to each distinct person of the Trinity and thus non-communicable (not shared in) by the other two divine persons.

principle. To be fair to Augustine, he never proclaimed that the word '*Filioque*' ('*and the Son*') should be inserted into the Nicene-Constantinopolitan Creed. However, he was referred to as one of the highest authorities by those later Latin Scholastic theologians who finally succeeded in interpolating it into the Creed.

St. Photius the Great, the ninth century Patriarch of Constantinople, in his famous *Mystagogy of the Holy Spirit*, explains the fundamental theological issue concerning the *Filioque* dispute between Roman Catholicism and the Orthodox East:

> If the Spirit, Who proceeds from the Father, proceeds also from the Son, what would prevent the immutability [i.e., unchangeability] of the hypostatic [i.e., personal] properties from necessarily foundering?… the Father … would survive as a mere name, since the property which characterizes Him would now be common, and the two hypostases of the God-head would coalesce into one person. And thus Sabellius or rather some other semi-Sabellian monster, would again sprout up among us.[39]

Ultimately, the three Persons of the Holy Trinity, and even each and every human person created in the image and likeness of

---

[39] St. Photius of Constantinople, *On the Mystagogy of the Holy Spirit, 9*, trans. Holy Transfiguration Monastery (Boston: Studion Publishers, 1983), 73. St. Photius writes elsewhere, "If indeed the Son is begotten from the Father, but the Spirit proceeds from the Son, according to their own opinion, will not impiety relegate the Spirit to the position of grandson and turn the tremendous mystery of our theology into protracted nonsense?" (*Mystagogy* 61, Ibid., 96).

God, is a mystery that must be experienced and not intellectually categorized. To subordinate the 'person' or 'personhood' to nature is more of a rational and logical way of attempting to define and understand the mystery of personhood. Augustine, in choosing this philosophical, rational, and ultimately anthropocentric approach, places an ontological priority on nature over person and thereby considers 'person' or 'personhood' in more of a psychological rather than a truly theological perspective.

Furthermore, Augustine shows his estrangement from the Orthodox East in his de-personalization of the Holy Spirit. He considers the Holy Spirit as more of an abstract concept, such as the bond, the communion, the gift, or the love shared between the Father and the Son,[40] rather than as a divine Person or distinct 'hypostasis' of the Holy Trinity. He clearly upholds the double procession[41] of the Holy Spirit.[42] He further blurs the personal distinctions in the Holy Trinity by claiming that the Holy Spirit proceeds from both the Father and the Son as from 'one principle.'[43] Clearly, Augustine has little appreciation for the personal or 'hypostatic' distinction of each unique divine Person of the Holy Trinity.

What then is at stake with this issue of Augustine's de-personalization of the Holy Trinity? What are the consequences of placing a priority on the abstract essence of God? In the ninth century, when the *Filioque* dispute became a serious and divisive issue between the Greek East and the Latin

---

[40] E.g., *On the Trinity* 15. 17 (27, 29) , 19 (33, 36, 37).

[41] Double procession, meaning that the Holy Spirit proceeds from the Father and the Son.

[42] *On the Trinity*, 15. 26 (45, 47).

[43] Ibid. 5. 14 (15).

West, the *Filioque* was referred to as the "crown of all evils."[44] Why is this? Why would the *Filioque* be seen as such a theological danger that could threaten the theological and spiritual vision of Christianity?

Could what we are witnessing today in Christianity be related to this theological error? After Vatican II, Roman Catholicism, in many ways, has floundered into theological and spiritual disarray. Many of its monasteries and parishes are embracing an over-secularization and a subjectivism which consider belief in a single God—even in one philosophical "supreme essence"—to have the same spiritual validity as Christian belief in the Holy Trinity. Some Catholic monasteries have embraced the techniques of meditation, such as Zen Buddhism and Hinduism, even offering books from gurus and Buddhist monks for sale in their bookstores.

If we lose the patristic *vision* of the three divine and distinct Persons of the Father, the Son, and the Holy Spirit, we lose the patristic *experience* of the Holy Trinity as well. Ultimately the mystery of the Holy Trinity cannot be *explained;* it can only be *experienced.* Attempts at rational explanations usually end in confusion and often in erroneous definitions.

The dogma of the Holy Trinity is not something that is merely believed in—it must also be *lived out* and *experienced* through one's personal participation in the ascetical, liturgical, and sacramental life of the Holy Church. We must not attempt to rationally speculate on our faith in the Holy Trinity. Rather we must *live it.* Only in this way does the therapeutic and transformative experience of the living God become a reality for the believer.

---

[44] See Photius the Great, *Encyclical to the Eastern Patriarchs* 8.

The tri-personal unity of the Holy Trinity is the unshakable foundation of the Orthodox Church and the ultimate ground of all existence.[45] Affirming the Persons of the Holy Trinity affirms and indeed *fulfills* our own personhood—which is made in the image of God.

Augustine's Christology

With this introduction to the divergent approaches to the mystery of the Holy Trinity, we proceed to a brief discussion on Augustine's Christology.

On first reading, much of Augustine's Christology seems to be soundly Orthodox. However, a closer reading of a few passages might cause great alarm to many Orthodox Christians.

The Definition of Chalcedon, which was officially formulated at the Fourth Ecumenical Council in 451, defines Orthodox Christology. It states, in part:

> One and the same Christ, Son, Lord, Only-begotten, made known in two natures [which exist] without confusion, without change, without division, without separation; the difference of the natures having been in no wise taken away by reason of the union, but rather the properties of each being preserved, and [both] concurring into one Person and one hypostasis—not parted or divided into two persons, but one and the same Son and Only-begotten, the divine Logos, the Lord Jesus Christ....[46]

---

[45] See Lossky, *Mystical Theology*, 65-66.

[46] Quoted in Alois Grillmeier, *Christ in Eastern Christian Tradition,*

To suggest that Christ took to Himself "a human person" is clearly Nestorian. The Nestorian heresy stressed the distinctions of the two natures in Christ at the expense of the unity of His one Person. This distinction was over-emphasized to the point of implying *two separate persons* in Christ. Such a teaching can lead ultimately to another ancient heresy called adoptionism, which taught that Jesus Christ is not the Son of God by nature, but the adopted Son of God by grace. Yet, this seems to be what Augustine infers in several places:

> For it was by this grace that a man, without any antecedent merit, was at the very commencement of His existence as man, so united in one person with the Word of God, that the very person Who was Son of man was at the same time Son of God, and the very person Who was Son of God was at the same time Son of man; and in the *adoption* of His human nature into the divine, the grace itself became in a way so natural to the man, as to leave no room for the entrance of sin.[47]

One Augustinian scholar highlights the adoptionist language often used by Augustine,

> In his earlier works, as throughout his life, Augustine speaks of the Word as 'bearing' or 'acting through' a human person … or as having 'put on' human flesh or human nature like a garment….[48]

---

trans. J.S. Bowden (New York: Sheed and Ward, 1965), 544.

[47] Augustine, Bishop of Hippo, *Enchiridion on Faith, Hope, and Love* (South Bend: Gateway Editions, 1961), 50-51 [italics added].

[48] Fitzgerald, *Augustine Through the Ages*, 167.

Whatever one's interpretation of Augustine's Christology, the unity of the Person of Christ does not seem to be as ontologically concrete as it is for the Fathers of the Orthodox East. Augustine's underdeveloped view of person again seems to be a cause of not only linguistic errors, but also a lack of theological clarity concerning the union of the Person of Christ. The question is raised: If the union in Christ is not a hypostatic union (i.e., a union through His Person), how are the two natures united in Christ? A further lack of clarity is conveyed in Augustine's *Enchiridion*:

> Now here the grace of God is displayed with the greatest power and clearness. For what merit had the human nature in the man Christ earned, that it should in this unparalleled way be taken up into the unity of the person of the only Son of God?... Now wherefore was this unheard of glory conferred on human nature—a glory which, as there was no antecedent merit, was of course wholly of grace—except that here those who looked at the matter soberly and honestly might behold a clear manifestation of the power of God's free grace, and might understand that they are justified from their sins by the same grace which made the man Christ Jesus free from the possibility of sin?[49]

From the Orthodox perspective, the Chalcedonian Definition is the summit of balance and perfection in understanding

---

[49] Augustine, *Enchiridion* 36, op.cit., 45-46. In all fairness to Augustine, his language seems clearly Orthodox in *Enchiridion* 35.

not only the hypostatic union in Christ, but also God's plan in creating the world and how He saves it by uniting it to Himself.

St. Maximus, writing in the seventh century, was the undisputed champion of the Chalcedonian Definition which he saw as the foundation for all the fullness of the complete cosmic experience of the Incarnation of Christ:

> He Who by the sheer inclination of His will laid the foundation of all creation, visible and invisible, had an ineffably good plan for created beings long before the ages. The plan was to mingle, without change on His part, with human nature by true hypostatic union.[50]

Orthodox Christology provides a unified worldview which is completely centered on the Person of Christ. And it is the Definition of Chalcedon which most clearly safeguards the heart of this message. In Christ, man and creation are raised to the Throne of God by a true *theanthropic* (or 'divine-human') union based on the Person of Christ. This union *deifies* man, and by extension, all of God's creation. Yet at the same time it preserves the distinction and inherent integrity of man's created nature from the uncreated nature of God. The Definition of Chalcedon thus provides the theological foundation for the spiritual experience which Augustine seldom refers to—man's personal experience as a true "partaker of divine nature."[51] Consequently for the Orthodox Church, salvation must be seen through the broader and more inclusive lens of

---

[50] *Questions to Thalassios,* 55, quoted from Blowers, *Exegesis and Spiritual Pedagogy in Maximus the Confessor,* 129.

[51] See II Peter 1:4.

deification or *theosis*, rather than being constricted merely to the juridical notion of divine justification.

St. Augustine's focus is centered more on the specific aspect of the sacrifice of the *Cross,* rather than on the organic wholeness of Christ's one undivided life, including His Incarnation, Transfiguration, Death, Resurrection, Ascension, and Second Coming. In a few isolated passages, Augustine did speak of deification.[52] Yet it was by no means an essential element of his experience of Christ. Augustine was more preoccupied with the notion of man's justification from what would later become known in Western Christianity as 'Original Sin.'

For Augustine, the divine image according to which man was originally created was now, on account of the Fall of Adam, almost completely destroyed through sin. As a result, all men are guilty of the consequences of Adam's Original Sin, and thus all men deserve eternal punishment. Such beliefs led Augustine to teach that unbaptized children are destined to hell, yet only lightly punished.[53] This taint in man of Original Sin, or 'Original Guilt,' distorts Augustine's view of human nature and its inherent potential in Christ.

In stark contrast to this perspective, the Orthodox Church considers Christ, the God-man, as the Archetype and the model for God's entire creation. The Person of Christ shows forth the unity of the uncreated God and created human nature, whereby the distinct character of each nature is preserved. St. Maximus writes,

> God made us so that we might become "partakers of the divine nature" (II Pet. 1:4) and sharers

---

[52] E.g., *On the Psalms* 49.1.2 and *Sermons* 192.1.1.
[53] E.g., *On Baptism* 1. 21, *et al.*

in His eternity, and so that we might come to
be like Him (1 John 3:2) through deification by
grace. It is through deification that all things are
reconstituted and achieve their permanence; and
it is for its sake that what is not is brought into
being and given existence.[54]

It is clear that Augustine's teachings concerning human
nature (including Original Guilt, the nature of grace, the Fall,
and predestination) have all influenced his understanding of
Christ's redemptive work. The teaching on Original Guilt, for
example, sets such spiritual limitations on human nature that
it necessitates a redemption based on principles of legalism.
The focus of Christ's saving work becomes overtly juridical
and is now centered not so much on freeing man from the
bonds of spiritual illness and death, but more on the inherited
guilt which all men have received from Adam at the moment
of their conception.

This truncating of the Orthodox understanding of salvation as deification was only reinforced by Augustine's speculations concerning the nature of grace and his lack of an essence/
energy distinction. Consequently, if man cannot participate in
God's deifying energies or uncreated grace (since Augustine
does not consider grace as 'uncreated'), man and God remain
forever separated. Thus salvation is not seen as a communion
and union (i.e., deification) with God which fulfills human
nature, but rather one that is reduced to a moral and juridical
relationship, the essential concern of which is ultimately pro-
nouncing one "not guilty."

---

[54] St. Maximus the Confessor, *Various Texts* 1. 42, quoted from Palmer
(London: Sherrard and Ware, 1981), 173.

Conclusion: Augustine's View of Man

It becomes clear then, when comparing the theology of the Augustinian West and patristic Orthodox East that one's view of man and his state, both before and after the Fall, will directly affect how one perceives man's *redemption* and what he is saved *from*. Sadly, Augustine's view of man after the Fall is considered by many to be not only un-Orthodox, but also reprehensible. Augustine calls the race of Adam

> a mass of slime; a mass of sin, of sins, of iniquity; a mass of wrath, of death, of damnation; of offense; a mass totally vitiated, damnable, damned.[55]

Augustine and his followers claimed that man is beyond healing, placing a curse on mankind which incapacitates the true God-given potential of human nature even in its fallen state.

Augustine taught that,

> The entire mass [of mankind], therefore, incurs penalty and if the deserved punishment of condemnation were rendered to all, it would without doubt be righteously rendered. They, therefore, who are delivered therefrom by grace are called, not vessels of their own merits, but 'vessels of mercy....' *The man who correctly appreciated the whole subject could not possibly blame the justice of God in wholly condemning all men whatsoever.*[56]

---

[55] Portalie, *A Guide to the Thought*, 212. All of these words are directly drawn from Augustine's writings.

[56] Augustine, *On Nature and Grace, Nicene and Post Nicene Fathers*, vol. 5, ch. 5, 123 [italics added].

It is clear that in Augustine's thought, all men are already doomed to perdition even before they are born.[57] Again (as was seen in his triadology) Augustine places a priority of nature over person, making man a slave under the tyranny of nature's fatalistic kingship. Beginning with the presupposition that all men are guilty, he has cast the darkest cloud possible over each and every human person created in the image of God. He states clearly that all of humanity is destined for hell, except the "elect," who are "predestined" for salvation by God's inscrutable will.[58]

The Orthodox Church, however, upholds and proclaims the inherent dignity and potential holiness of every human person, even in our fallen state.

In Augustine's theological system, it seems that salvation is not a synergy of man's restored will working with God's, but rather only God working His will through man. We also note that in Augustine's Christology the concept of the human will seems to remain unaffected by the Incarnation. St. John Chrysostom noted that Christ came "not to destroy human

---

[57] "…those who were unable to believe because they were mere infants and who perished, dying without receiving the washing of regeneration by which alone they could be set free from Original Guilt; all these are not separated from that mass which, all agree, is condemned, since all men are bound for damnation because of one man's fault" (*On Rebuke and Grace,* 12-14, quoted from Henry Bettenson, *The Later Christian Fathers* [Oxford: Oxford University Press, 1970], 210).

[58] "Therefore when God promised to Abraham in his seed the faith of the nations, saying, 'I have established thee a father of many nations,' whence the apostle says, 'Therefore it is of faith, that the promise, according to grace, might be established to all the seed,' *He promised not from the power of our will but from His own predestination*" (Augustine, *On Predestination of the Saints,* in *The Fathers of the Church,* "Four Anti-Pelagian Writings," vol. 1, 19 [italics added]).

nature but to set man's free choice aright."[59] Yet Augustine clearly taught that man had lost the will to do good after the Fall:

> For it was by the evil use of his free-will that man destroyed both it and himself ... so, *when man by his own free-will sinned, then sin being victorious over him, the freedom of his will was lost.*[60]

It seems that such a stark view of human nature, and in particular of the innate dignity of human *freedom,* may not be unrelated to the widespread rejection of Christianity by countless multitudes, as well as the reactionary stance of our modern society against basic Christian values and teaching.

In conclusion, St. Augustine has indeed left a major impact on the world that we live in today. Augustine's thinking has influenced much of Western theology, philosophy, spirituality, and literature. In attempting to better understand what Augustine wrote and taught, we can locate and see the germs of thought that may not only have affected our society but even our *own thinking.* In seeking to understand his theological and philosophical principles which continue to undergird and govern many aspects of modern thought, we can hopefully be liberated not only from them, but also from the overreactions that they may produce.

Many more areas could have been addressed and discussed in this work. Nonetheless, it is hoped that the few issues raised here suffice to show how Augustine's theological method is

---

[59] St. John Chrysostom, *Homily on Romans,* 11, *Nicene and Post Nicene Fathers,* vol. 10, 410.

[60] Augustine, *Enchiridion,* 30.

indeed different from, and largely foreign to, the Orthodox patristic tradition.

We can only surmise that Augustine spent much of his time writing, for his works fill an amazing sixteen full volumes of Migne's *Patrology*.[61] His thought was not always borne of experience but more so in philosophical speculations which were at times alien to the common mind and life of the Church.

Augustine's incomparable genius has earned him a place in history that is without precedent and beyond compare. Whether one agrees with him, or reacts against him, Western Christianity and its culture has been shaped by the hand of St. Augustine of Hippo.

---

[61] Tellingly, Augustine had two complete volumes called *Retractions*.

SERMON ON THE DORMITION
OF THE MOTHER OF GOD

IN THE NAME of the Father, and of the Son, and of the Holy Spirit. Amen.

When we hear someone speak about the Ark of the Covenant from the Old Testament, oftentimes we think of modern depictions, of movies, or books, and especially the biblical accounts that present us with a fearful, awesome, and even wrathful picture. We recall that above this wooden box, which was covered with pure gold, God spoke with Moses from the mercy seat in between the two cherubim. The Ark would often go in front of the people of Israel in battles, terrifying and destroying enemies, but also assuring the Israelites of God's blessing, of His power, and of their victory. Those who tampered with the Ark became ill or even died.

How then might we, who are grass and made of earthen clay, begin to discourse and contemplate the living Ark of God, the Most-holy Theotokos, who was the fulfillment and the awesome reality of which the Ark of the Old Testament was merely a shadow? It is interesting that this Feast falls, not coincidentally, at a time when many people are on a vacation or are too busy for the Church, since they are readying themselves for seemingly more important things, such as the coming school year. Why is this?

This present awesome and glorious mystery is something which is not a subject for speculation, for human logic, or for vain tampering. It is a tremendous mystery that is hidden and only revealed when it is humbly received from within the light of the depths of the Church's tradition. This Feast is immensely joyful and life-giving for those who with child-like faith and without argument seek to enter into its festivities. Contrastingly, for those who are outside, subject to the Law of the Old Covenant and are without the grace of the New, it is a dark mountain which is incomprehensible and even fearful. But for those who have prepared themselves with fasting and prayer and by being present at today's festivities, the tomb of the Mother of God is joy; it is life and it is a light-covered mountain for our spiritual ascent today.

How could her tomb be anything else than an inexhaustible fountain of life, when she herself was the spring which poured forth the living life-giving water which is Christ Himself? How could her body know corruption, having borne within it the Son of God, Who shone with unbearable light on Mount Tabor? She is that bush which Moses saw which burned with the immaterial and inconceivable fire of the God-head without being consumed. She is the new Eve, the mother of the eternal life which was Christ our God. Her soul and body were full of grace, so filled with the life of God and of holiness that it was not possible for them to be consigned to darkness, death, and decay. She is the living Paradise who had within herself the Tree of Life, and she is the window through which shines into this world the ineffable light of the Triune God.

Today she, like the Ark of the Old Covenant, goes before us as a banner of victory, a wall of defense and forerunner of the fulfillment of all of God's promises to all mankind. Having now crossed the frontier which separates us from the age to come, through her bodily ascent to heaven, she has become the highest of all creation, and the realization of the end for which humanity was created. She is the fulfillment of all beauty and virtue and is a universal advocate for all before the throne of God, now and at the Second Coming.

What then does this Feast seek to reveal to us today? How can we grasp something of its immense depth and profundity? Simply put, this Feast is a reminder for us all that when we, through God's grace, live a life of holiness, as our foremost example the Theotokos did, and when we like her keep Christ's word in our hearts and do His will, we will according to the word of the Lord Himself, "never see death" (John 8:51). When we, by keeping to the narrow way, become filled with God's own Life, our death will not be a death but a translation to a new and better life; we will go from life to life and, if we can become like the saints even to a small degree, our death will become a source of joy and life for those who come after us.

This narrow way that the Church exhorts us to follow, as we all know, is the call to a life of repentance. This repentance is not feigned, or morose and depressed, but rather it is an attitude of our hearts, always willing and ready to change for the sake of following God and His commandments and for the good of others. It is an attitude which always is ready to ask for forgiveness; to humble oneself and to accept words of instruction or even criticism from others.

The repentance which brings life and holiness is one which never lets go of the hem of Christ's garments but clings to Him in prayer and hope, ceaselessly crying out, "I am Thine; save me" (Ps. 118:94 LXX), and "Lord ... speak the word only, and my servant [i.e., my soul] shall be healed" (Matt. 8:8). A life of repentance never abandons Christ the Physician, though it may fall every hour, but constantly turns back to the Lord in prayer and humbles itself amidst its sins, sorrows, and misfortunes. It never will leave the only One Who has the power to forgive and heal it, to bring about its restoration and establishment in every good thing.

O my brethren in Christ, let us consider this awesome wonder! The Ark of the Old Testament went before the people of Israel as they were coming out of the desert into the Promised Land being led by the Prophet Joshua; and today, the Theotokos, the living Ark, goes before us into the Promised Land of Heaven as our forerunner and prototype, as we are led by Jesus Christ, Whom Joshua of old dimly prefigured. Then, the Ark parted the waters of the Jordan so that the people could pass through into the Promised Land; but now, the Theotokos, through her intercessions, parts the often tumultuous waters of our lives so that we can safely pass through and enter into the Kingdom on high.

In the Old Testament, the Second Book of Maccabees tells us that the Ark disappeared and was hidden, being taken up into a high mountain by the Prophet Jeremiah, not to be seen or found by anyone, it is said, until God gathers all His people in the final times. Now, too, the living life-giving Ark of the New Covenant has been taken from among us, ascending bodily into heaven after her death so that she might be the first-fruits of the creation through whom we can receive every good thing, being our supreme and ever-present advocate after God and our invincible Protectress who is terrifying to our enemies.

Let us joyfully come forth today to venerate the life-giving tomb of the Mother of God. Through her prayers, with the help of all the saints, let us strive to imitate the Mother of God through our life of humble repentance through which we, like the Good Thief, may steal Paradise, unworthy though we may be, so that together we might glorify Almighty God: the Father, the Son, and the Holy Spirit, to Whom belongs worship and glory forever. Amen.

SERMON ON THE EXALTATION
OF THE LIFE-GIVING CROSS

IN THE NAME of the Father, and of the Son, and of the Holy Spirit. Amen.

Today we commemorate in this present Feast the finding of the Holy and Precious Cross of Christ by St. Helena in Jerusalem in the 4th century. St. Isaac of Syria tells us that just as the Presence and Glory of God dwelt within the wood of the Ark in the Old Testament, so also this same Glory and Power of God now resides in the Holy Wood of the Cross. The glory that departed from the Ark of the Old Covenant entered into the Holy Cross of the New Covenant on which the Lord was enthroned when He was crucified. Hence, we bow down, as the hymn says, "in worship before the Cross" because we recognize that the glory (or the *Shekinah*) of God and the Wood of the Cross have been inseparably joined.

As St. John of Damascus explains: "I do not venerate the matter but I venerate the Creator of matter, Who became matter for me, Who condescended to live in matter, and Who, through matter accomplished my salvation; I do not cease to respect the matter through which my salvation is accomplished."[1] The hymns of today's service exhort us: "Be glad, O heaven, and rejoice, O earth! The all-holy Cross cometh forth, sanctifying with grace us who venerate it as a well-spring of holiness and the cause of all deification..." for today at its exaltation, "the Cross of the Lord, which is venerated by the faithful, is seen to be as bright as the sun; and as we kiss it our souls are enlightened."

The Cross is not an ornament or a piece of jewelry but it is "the Way." It is the Way of Christ which is quintessentially a life of love and forgiveness. We are commanded to love our enemies—the Cross. We are commanded to do good to those who hate us—the Cross. We are commanded to pray for those who spit in our face—the Cross. If we have not love in our hearts, we have not God in our hearts, for God is love. The goal is God; the goal is to love. As Elder Sophrony says, "The bidding 'love your enemies,' is the 'fire on the earth' that the Lord brought by His coming ... and It is the Uncreated Divine Light which shone down on the Apostles on Mount Tabor."[2] This is the glory of the Cross.

It was in a garden and through a tree that man fell away from God; and it was in a garden and through the Tree of the Cross that God reconciled the creation to Himself, effectively healing mankind's Fall. Now we must appropriate and accept this gift of healing, for as Orthodox Christians we must not be sentimental spectators of the Cross, but rather participants of the life-giving death of Christ, crucifying our passions, selfishness, pettiness, and sinful inclinations that separate us from

---

[1] St. John of Damascus, *PG* 94:1245 AB, quoted from Scouteris, *Ecclesial Being*, 90.

[2] (Sakharov), *St. Silouan the Athonite.*

God and lead us to death. We must affix ourselves to the Cross by keeping the commandments of the Lord, remembering and accepting that the Cross is the narrow way which we all must go and which leads us to life and to the Kingdom of heaven. St. Isaac the Syrian tells us that the wisdom and "the knowledge of the Cross [are] concealed in the sufferings of the Cross. The more *our* participation in its sufferings, the greater the perception we gain through the Cross [into the mysteries of God.]"[3]

Indeed, to be an Orthodox Christian means that the principal way we learn about the creation, the Fall, salvation, and the world to come is through suffering. We don't pray for suffering but rather endure for the sake of Christ the sufferings that are the common lot of all mankind. This fallen world, St. Maximus tells us, is always in need of a Cross, a crucifixion. We must not accept the fallen world to be "natural and normal." This is the greatest lie that is perpetrated on us by the media, the passions, and the devil, for it excuses sin instead of making us realize change is possible and that we need to work for that change.

The only ones who are really natural and normal are the saints. The rest of us are in dire need of the Cross which we must use as a ladder and a tool to restore our nature to its heavenly, holy, normal, and natural state. In hindsight, we will see that the suffering we endure when we follow the Lord has great benefits for us: it can draw us closer to God, enables us to have empathy and concern for others, and helps us to stay

---

[3] St. Isaac the Syrian, *Ascetical Homilies of Saint Isaac the Syrian,* Homily 74, trans. Holy Transfiguration Monastery (Boston: Holy Transfiguration Monastery, 1984) [italics added].

away from sin, for as St. Peter says, "he that has suffered in the flesh has ceased from sin" (1 Pet. 4:1).

And yet, while we are going through trials and tribulations, we may be perplexed and in despair. However, this is precisely how patience and character is instilled within us; therefore, we must not become fainthearted. Through this acceptance of trials and tribulations with faith, we begin to acquire humility, which St. John Climacus says is the mother of perfection.

In conclusion, we can recall that it was on this day that St. John Chrysostom died 1601 years ago. His Feast is transferred to November 13th in order that it might be celebrated with due honor and solemnity. How fitting that one who suffered so dearly for Christ, and died in exile, carrying his Cross over the regions of Asia Minor, reminds us today: We must not just read about the Cross and the Crucifixion but rather we must hold the remembrance of them "deeply in our hearts: the crown of thorns, the robe, the reed, the blows, the nails, the spitting, and the mockery." He says that these things, if continually meditated on and recalled, "are sufficient *to take down all anger*,"[4] which is the primary obstacle to love, the wicked offspring of pride and one of the main reasons why grace cannot enter and abide in our hearts; it is, as St. Theophan says, the fire of hell. St. John Chrysostom says that "if we are mocked and suffer injustice [e.g., trials, suffering, and difficulties], we must say 'the servant is not greater than his Lord.'"[5] For we recall, as the Scripture explains, that we must through great tribulations enter into the Kingdom of heaven.

[4] St. John Chrysostom, *Homily 84*, in *Nicene and Post Nicene Fathers*, vol. 14, 315.
[5] Ibid.

My brethren, there is no other way to the Kingdom of heaven but through our own personal Cross. Our Cross can become sweet and fragrant with life, like the flowers that surround the Cross in front of us, if we endure it for the sake of the love of God. Let us endure it bravely, with a freely chosen courage, hoping in God's mercy that if we endure with Him, we shall also live and reign with Him, for we have no continuing city here. Let us call heaven our home and let us endeavor with all our might to imitate the King Who showed us the way. For, "Today [as the hymns of the Church tell us,] the Cross is exalted and the world is sanctified. For Thou, O Christ, Who art enthroned with the Father and the Holy Spirit hast spread Thine arms upon it, and drawn the world to the knowledge of Thee. Make worthy of divine glory those that have put their trust in Thee." Amen.

Sermon on the Sunday of Orthodoxy

In the Name of the Father, and of the Son, and of the Holy Spirit. Amen.

Beginning in the reign of Leo iii in the 8th century and ending in the reign of Theophilus in the 9th century, the Church of Christ was troubled by the persecution of the iconoclasts: those who hated icons. After Theophilus' death, his widow, the Empress St. Theodora, together with the Patriarch St. Methodius, established Orthodoxy anew. This ever-memorable Queen venerated the icon of the Mother of God in the presence of the Patriarch and the other confessors and righteous men, and openly cried out these holy words: "If anyone does not offer veneration to the holy icons, *not* adoring them as though they were gods, but venerating them out of love as images of the archetype, let him be anathema."

With common prayer and fasting during the whole first week of the Forty-day Fast of Great Lent, she asked God's forgiveness for her husband. After this, on the first Sunday of the Great Fast, she and her son, Michael the Emperor, made a procession with all the clergy and people and restored the holy icons, again adorning the Church of Christ with them.

Since time immemorial, the Church has venerated and loved the image of her beloved Lord, God, and Savior, Jesus Christ. We see this borne out from early Church historical accounts to the present day, for the icon is a testimony and confirmation that "God was manifest in the flesh ... seen of angels, preached unto the Gentiles, believed on in the world, received up into glory" (1 Tim. 3:16). Indeed, the icon reveals that it was *this* world that the Lord made His flesh, sanctifying it, restoring it from the inside out, filling it with His incorruptible Divinity, and raising it to the Throne of God. This is the dignity which you and I share, being made in His image, through baptism, which we must enter more deeply into through living our life for Him Who gave His life for us.

St. John of Damascus tells us that "in times past, God, without body and form, could in no way be represented [hence, the prohibition of images in the Old Testament]. But now, since God has appeared in the flesh and lived among men, I can depict that which is visible of God [for Christ is 'the image of the invisible God' (Col. 1:15)]."[1] In Christ we find the fullest affirmation of the innate goodness of matter which now can be the medium of divine energy and grace.

Icons of Christ, of the saints, and of the Mother of God are a pledge of the coming victory of a redeemed cosmos over a fallen one, showing forth a restoration of the world back to its original purpose: to glorify its Creator. In the icon we see a concrete example of matter restored through grace in the life

---

[1] St. John of Damascus, *On the Holy Icons.*

of the Church to its original harmony and beauty. Matter now serves as a vessel of the grace of the All-holy Spirit.

As we commemorate the Sunday of Orthodoxy, we are not merely remembering an event of ages past, but rather we are professing the triumph of Truth over heresy which the icon proclaims. Theologically, what is heresy but a distortion of the true and correct vision of God, which is salvation? And what is dogma but the words that describe that vision of Who God is and what He is really like? For the Orthodox, salvation is this vision of God. Many of the saints of our Church, from St. Paul to St. Silouan, saw Christ in His glory; through this vision they were altered in the fabric of their being, and through it were saved.

We represent in image Christ our God and Lord so that the Incarnation is shown forth as real and true, and not a phantasm or ghost. But even more so, we do this to show forth the face of God which reveals the pledge of the vision of God: this is salvation. The veneration of the image of Christ is the pledge and our beginning to our own personal experience of the vision of the glory of God in the face of Jesus Christ.

Therefore, my brethren, let us venerate the icon of the Savior, of the saints, and of the Mother of God and thereby proclaim the inherent goodness of the entire creation: of its redemption, restoration, and transfiguration through the Incarnation of Christ. It is now our turn to offer our own personal world as a Eucharistic sacrifice, redeeming and transfiguring the material world which we inhabit through our prayer, our fasting, and our thanksgiving to our Creator Who sustains us, enlightens us, and saves us through the incalculable Treasury of our Orthodox Faith which we have been given and which we celebrate today.

The Triumph of Orthodoxy happens in my personal life when Christ becomes incarnate through my keeping of the commandments. Orthodoxy triumphs when I become an icon of Christ through my love and kindness to all those I encounter, being a vessel of His Presence. Orthodoxy triumphs when the falsehood of my passions are denounced and demolished and Christ is enthroned as King and God in my heart. Today is the first day of the rest of Great Lent. Let us fortify ourselves by abstaining from meat, from sin, and from devouring our neighbor with our criticism. Let us glorify God in the short time we have remaining in our life by doing works of charity, alms, and prayer. Let us build up the Church and one another, placing our time and talents into those things which will benefit us eternally. Let us give thanks to God Who has brought us here today, having given us the Treasury of the Orthodox Faith, of that Gift of the undistorted vision of God which is salvation for the world. The Triumph of Orthodoxy is the Triumph of the Only True and Living Way which leads the entire race of mankind to salvation. Let us enter more deeply into it, embrace it, confess it, and fervently live our Orthodoxy through the grace and mercy of our God: Father, Son and Holy Spirit, to Whom be all glory and honor, now and forever. Amen.

SERMON ON THE SUNDAY OF ALL SAINTS

IN THE NAME of the Father, and of the Son, and of the Holy Spirit. Amen.

Today, on this first Sunday after Pentecost, the Church celebrates the commemoration of all the saints known and unknown, who have been sanctified by God; who have pleased Him and who now stand before His Throne in the heavenly Sion. All of us are called to this glory, "called to be saints" as St. Paul says in his Epistle to the Romans (1:7); and yet not all respond to this call. That is to say, not all people wish to do the will of Him Who wills all men to be saved. However, most do not realize Who and what they are rejecting by failing to pursue those eternal things which are above.

It is through the saints that we can come to see that our call in Christ Jesus is real and that it is very possible for us, no matter who we are and what we've done and where we are today, to become like they are: exceedingly precious vessels of the Holy Spirit.

We know that in Antioch during the time of St. John Chrysostom in the 4th century, this Feast was already being celebrated on the same day that it is today, the first Sunday after Pentecost. It was primarily established to honor all of the martyrs who witnessed to Christ in the early persecutions before Christianity was legalized by St. Constantine in 313. However, this commemoration, falling as it does immediately after the Descent of the Holy Spirit at Pentecost, reminds us of something very important—that it is the Holy Spirit Who makes saints, and that without the Holy Spirit, as Christ tells us, we can do nothing.

Without the One Who sanctifies the work of those who trust in Him, it is not possible for anyone to become a saint, and that without Him we are merely, in the words of St. Silouan, "sinful clay." Elder Sophrony tells in his biography about St. Silouan that "a single saint is an extraordinarily precious phenomenon for all mankind. By the mere fact of their existence—unknown, maybe, to the world but known to God—the saints draw down on the world, on all humanity, a great benediction from God."[1]

We are all called to be saints and yet not all respond to this call. To become a saint is to fulfill the will of Him Who created us in His image. It could and should even be considered the normal course for a Christian's life: that is, to become a saint, participating in God's likeness; being like unto Him in all things; and even sharing His eternal and uncreated Life. "To many people the saints seem far removed from us. But the saints are far only from people who have distanced themselves, they are very close to them that keep Christ's commandments."[2] By coming into contact with the saints through

---

[1] (Sakharov), *Saint Silouan the Athonite*, 223.

[2] Ibid, 394.

prayer, through venerating their relics, and through their icons, we actually come into contact with the Lord Himself Who dwells in and rests in His saints.

Through reading the *Lives of the Saints*, we can become inspired to do the will of God, to cast off our limitations, and to stretch beyond what we feel and think is possible. It is through the saints we see that with God all things are possible; that man does not live by bread alone, and that the high calling in Jesus Christ is possible for everyone whether a harlot, like St. Mary of Egypt, an Emperor, like St. Justinian, or even a humble parent, like St. Macrina and St. Gregory. We are all called to be saints no matter who we are, no matter where we are, and no matter what we do, and yet not all respond to this call.

Saints are not merely just good people, doing the good things, but rather, as St. John Maximovitch tells us, their holiness and sanctity "is not simply righteousness ... but the saints have such a height of righteousness that they are so filled with the grace of God that it flows from them and out upon those who are in fellowship with them. Great is their blessedness, *which proceeds from the vision of the Glory of God.* Filled to overflowing also with a love for men which proceeds from love for God, they are responsive to the needs of men and to their supplications, and become mediators and intercessors for them before God."[3]

The Fathers tell us that "the glory which the Lord gives His saints is so exceedingly great that if men were to see a saint as he really is, they would fall on their faces in veneration,

---

[3] Valerii Lukianov, *Lantern of Grace: Seven Homilies in Memory of Our Father Among the Saints, John, Archbishop of Shanghai and San Francisco,* trans. Isaac; Lambertson (Howell: Diocese of Western America of the Russian Orthodox Church Outside Russia), 70.

unable to bear the manifestation of the heavenly Glory."[4] We are all called to be saints, and yet not all respond to this call, because the task is very difficult and the way is narrow. And astonishingly, it means that we never arrive at our goal, for God is infinite and this process of growth in sanctity will go on forever, even in eternity. However, the saints were the first to see not only their shortcomings but oftentimes considered themselves to be the worst of sinners, like St. Paul said in his First Epistle to Timothy (1:15). This is because they did not think themselves merely bad or even good for that matter. No, it was because they saw the vision of Christ God in His glory and through this heavenly contact, the depth and reality of the fallen state of mankind was revealed to them in all of its tragedy and horror.

We are all called to be saints and yet not all of us respond to this call. If we *are* to respond to this call, we must order our hearts and our lives so as to seek to encounter the One Who Is, the Almighty, the First and the Last, the One Who is everlasting, the One Who co-reigns with the Father and the Holy Spirit, our Lord Jesus Christ. If we strive for this, to know God and do His will, then there will *never, ever,* be a point in our spiritual life where we can say "I have given enough to God or to others for the sake of Christ."

Rather, in stark contrast, the closer we come to God, the more that we will feel as if we have not done enough, and as if we are constantly falling short of becoming what we are called to be. If and when we feel self-satisfied, or that we have given enough to God and to others for His sake, it is then that we are in bad shape. We do not see the truth of our spiritual state,

----

[4] (Sakharov), *Saint Silouan the Athonite,* 223.

and we are fooled by our apparent "goodness," and sadly, the Fathers of the Church teach us that we are far from the Kingdom of heaven. For there is only One that is Good, and that One is God, Who bestows and shares His goodness with all of mankind.

We have all fallen short of attaining the full stature of Christ. We have all made mistakes. Nevertheless, the first and ever continuing step on the path to becoming saints is repentance, turning from ourselves to God; not arrogantly imagining that we have found God's favor. But we ever seek it, confessing Christ through our lives and our actions. We are all called to be saints. Let not one of us reject this call through imagining we have attained something already, but forgetting those things which are behind, let us all press onward towards the goal of the high calling which is in Jesus Christ our Lord to Whom be all glory and honor, now and forever. Amen.

SERMON ON THE
CANAANITE WOMAN

IN THE NAME of the Father, and of the Son, and of the Holy Spirit. Amen.

There once was a young man who was called upon to take care of a sick and sometimes very unpleasant dying old man. This young man was inexperienced with such work but sought eagerly to help the elder, always seeking to maintain goodwill and loving concern in his heart for the dying one. One day, at a time when the older man was nearing death, he began to be especially violent with his words, nearly bringing his younger helper to the point of a terrible despair. In a moment of mis-understanding, the elder man began to berate the young lad to the point of painful tears, almost striking him.

The younger one fled, feeling that a grave injustice had taken place. After weeping for an hour or so and recovering from the shock, the young man realized that their was no way that he was going to win. The injustice was never going to be set aright. The old man needed help, and the only way to be able to continue to help him was by asking his forgiveness.

With help from God, the young man came back to the room where the dying man lay and asked for his pardon for what had happened. At this, the elder accepted and told the young boy something that surprised and dazzled him. Peering up while coughing and wheezing, the elder stated: "If you can ask for forgiveness even when you are not at fault, there will always be hope for you."

Oftentimes in our lives we suffer what seem to be injustices, whether from the circumstances of our lives or from other people. We get sick, we suffer, we lose our jobs, we have others who hate us and speak poorly about us; this list could go on and on. It may even seem that at times, because of an agonizing loss in our lives, especially of a loved one, that even God Himself is unjustly punishing us.

In the Gospel today, we hear a wonderful and yet unusual story of a woman from Canaan; she represents in her person the Gentiles who would come to Christ. She explains of a terrible misfortune in her own life: Her daughter was possessed by a demon, a plight that can only be really understood when someone has actually experienced it. After the Lord heard her, the Gospel amazingly says that, "He answered her *not a word.*"

How many times has this happened to us? We beseech God for help; we tell Him of a terrible sorrow, difficulty, loss, or injustice; and, perplexingly, He answers us *not a word.* The language that God often uses when He speaks to us personally is the language of silence. It is a language that must elicit a particular response from us if we desire to continue our conversation with God: humility and patient perseverance. Often God allows us a period of waiting to show ourselves, and others, how we react and what we do in the face of difficulty, for it is only in adversity that virtue will be made manifest.

God loves us infinitely and because of this love He makes us wait. We live in a world that is a push-button, instant-internet-buying, fast-paced consumer society, conditioning us with sometimes unreasonable expectations. However, as the Lord reminds us, "My thoughts are not your thoughts and my ways are not your ways" (Isa. 55:8). The way to God, if we really wish to know Him, is down. The word Canaanite literally means "humility." This Canaanite (i.e., humble) woman, an image of 'going down,' after receiving the silence of the Lord perseveres in her requests as an image of faith and constancy. Perplexingly to us, because of it, she is actually rebuked by the Lord. He says "It is not meet to take the children's bread and give it to the dogs." And to this she replies, "Yea, Lord, yet even the dogs eat of the crumbs which fall from their master's table."

This dialogue may seem to be madness; even indignity may arise in our hearts when we read it. However, a very deep spiritual principle is being revealed to us if we wish to grasp hold and take it: this kind of humility is a divine virtue. Humility, St. Silouan says, is the light in which we behold the Unapproachable Light, which is God.[1] Just as our own lives come from outside ourselves (e.g., our parents), so humility can only be given to us from outside ourselves, usually through humiliation. Whatever we may encounter in our life, if we can humbly meet it with a certainty that God loves us, that God wills our salvation, and that somehow He is in control of everything (even the bad), then like the Canaanite woman we will be able to receive that precious gift of humility that enables us to have

---

[1] (Sakharov), *St. Silouan the Athonite*, 299.

our prayers answered before God. This makes us strong with His strength, and that will lead us to the Kingdom of heaven.

After the woman bows her head in humility at this stunning and unbelievable rebuke, the Lord pronounces her blessed and says, "'O woman, great is your faith! Be it unto you even as you desire.' And her daughter was made whole from that very hour." Christ loved her enough to test her, to humble her, to make her see her own inadequacy in dealing with the issue at hand.

We too, when we are crushed and when it seems that sorrow after sorrow and difficulty after difficulty fall upon us, must persevere in our dialogue with the Lord. It is only through a humble acceptance of the circumstances of our lives and a willingness to take responsibility for everything that has happened to us, with all of our failures, misfortunes, and sorrows, that we will be given the strength to overcome them, and through the mercy of God, to grow through them.

We must not nor can we ever despair by thinking that God will abandon us and that He is unmerciful and does not love us. The Christian message is opposite of that of the world: St. Paul tells us that the one "whom the Lord loves He chastens" (Heb. 12:6) to bring us to a greater knowledge of ourselves, to a greater likeness of His Son Who is the express image of humility, and also for a greater compassion and love for our fellow travelers that suffer similar trials. For there are two things we must always be certain of: God loves us and He wills our salvation, always granting in our life those things that bring us closer to Him and to salvation.

Injustices will certainly be present in our life. God will speak the great language of silence to us often. However, if we can bow our heads, and persevere in the midst of humiliation, trusting in the love of God which is in Christ Jesus our Lord, there will always be hope for us. Indeed, there will always be hope for us if in the midst of seeming injustice we can swallow our pride and take responsibility for it, most often by asking for forgiveness from God and from others, even when it is not our fault. To blame others is the way of the fallen world, but to take the blame upon ourselves is the way of Christ that leads us to Life. Indeed, there are no greater or more powerful words that we have within our immediate reach that epitomize the unfathomable depth of humility better than these: "Forgive me."

Let us learn of Christ Who is meek and lowly and we will find rest. Let us bow our head on our own cross and commit our souls into the hands of God and most certainly we will see our own resurrection, today and in the world to come. Amen.

A Prayer Rule[1]

Trisagion Prayers

In the Name of the Father, and of the Son, and of the Holy Spirit. Amen.

Glory to Thee, O God; glory to Thee.

O Heavenly King, the Comforter, the Spirit of Truth, Who art everywhere present and fillest all things; Treasury of blessings and Giver of Life: Come and abide in us, and cleanse us from every impurity, and save our souls, O Good One.

Holy God, Holy Mighty, Holy Immortal: have mercy on us. (*thrice*)

---

[1] A prayer rule must not and cannot be said in the car, but rather alone, in front of the icons and Gospel, preferably with a lit candle and, if possible, the room lights dimmed. It is important to remember that we will *never* have time for God but rather must *make* time for God, for the "Kingdom of heaven suffers violence, and the violent take it by force" (Matt. 11:12). The best time to pray is in the morning or in the evening, when it is darker.

Also, when using a rule of prayer we must be flexible and do what works for us; our goal is to maintain the connection with God and cultivate a real relationship, not just fulfill our 'rule' of prayer.

Glory to the Father, and to the Son, and to the Holy Spirit, now and ever, and unto the ages of ages. Amen.

O Most Holy Trinity, have mercy on us. O Lord, cleanse us from our sins. Master, pardon our iniquities. O Holy One, visit and heal our infirmities for Thy name's sake.

Lord, have mercy. (*thrice*)

Glory to the Father, and to the Son, and to the Holy Spirit, now and ever, and unto the ages of ages. Amen.

Our Father, Who art in the heavens, hallowed be Thy name. Thy kingdom come, Thy will be done, on earth as it is in heaven. Give us this day our daily bread, and forgive us our debts, as we forgive our debtors; and lead us not into temptation, but deliver us from the evil one.

Lord, have mercy. (*twelve times*)

Glory to the Father, and to the Son, and to the Holy Spirit, now and ever, and unto the ages of ages. Amen.

Come let us worship God our King. Come let us worship and fall down before Christ our King and God. Come let us worship and fall down before Christ Himself, our King and God.

Psalm 50

Have mercy on me, O God, according to Thy great mercy; and according to the multitude of Thy compassions blot out my transgression. Wash me thoroughly from mine iniquity, and cleanse me from my sin. For I know mine iniquity, and my sin is ever before me. Against Thee only have I sinned and done this evil before Thee, that Thou mightest be justified in Thy words, and prevail when Thou art judged. For behold, I was conceived in iniquities, and in sins did my mother bear me. For behold, Thou hast loved truth; the hidden and secret things of Thy wisdom hast Thou made manifest unto me. Thou shalt sprinkle me with hyssop, and I shall be made clean; Thou shalt wash me, and I shall be made whiter than snow. Thou shalt make me to hear joy and gladness, the bones that be humbled, they shall rejoice. Turn Thy face away from my sins, and blot out all mine iniquities. Create in me a clean heart, O God, and renew a right spirit within me. Cast me not away from Thy presence, and take not Thy Holy Spirit from me. Restore unto me the joy of Thy salvation, and with Thy governing Spirit establish me. I shall teach transgressors Thy ways, and the ungodly shall turn back unto Thee. Deliver me from blood-guiltiness, O God, Thou God of my salvation; my tongue shall rejoice in Thy righteousness. O Lord, Thou shalt open my lips, and my mouth shall declare Thy praise. For if Thou hadst desired sacrifice, I had given it; with whole-burnt offerings Thou shalt not be pleased. A sacrifice unto God is a broken spirit; a heart that is broken and humbled God will not despise. Do good, O Lord, in Thy good pleasure unto Sion, and let the walls of Jerusalem be builded. Then shalt Thou be pleased with a sacrifice of righteousness, with oblations and whole-burnt offerings. Then shall they offer bullocks upon Thine altar.

The Nicene-Constantinopolitan Creed

I believe in one God, (*Deut. 6:4, Isa. 48:17, 44:6*) **the Father Almighty,** (*Eph. 4:6*) **Maker of heaven and earth** (*Gen. 1:1, 1:26*) **and of all things visible and invisible.** (*Col. 1:16, Rom. 1:20*) **And in one Lord Jesus Christ,** (*Eph. 4:5, I Cor. 8:6*) **the Son of God,** (*Matt.16:16*) **the Only-begotten,** (*John 1:18, I John 5:1*) **begotten of**

the Father before all ages, (*John 1:1, 17:5*) **Light of Light,** (*John 1:4, 1:7-8, Acts 9:3, Tim. 6:16*) **True God of True God,** (*Col. 2:9, John 1:1, Mark 2:7, Micah 5:2, Isa. 9:6, 44:6, Rev 1:11*) **begotten,** (*I John 5:1*) **not made,** (*John 1:1, Heb. 7:3, John 8:58, 17:5, Phil. 2:6*) **of one essence with the Father,** (*John 10:30, I John 2:23*) **by whom all things were made;** (*John 1:3, 1:10, Col. 1:16*) **Who for us men and for our salvation** (*Matt. 1:21, Luke 2:30*) **came down from Heaven** (*John 3:13, 6:38*) **and was incarnate of the Holy Spirit and the Virgin Mary** (*Luke 1:35, Isa. 7:14*) **and became man.** (*John 1:14, I John 4:2*) **And was crucified for us under Pontius Pilate,** (*John 19:16*) **and suffered,** (*Ps. 21, Isa. 53, Matt. 27, Heb. 2:9*) **and was buried,** (*Luke 23:53*) **and on the third day rose again** (*Hos. 6:2, Matt. 28:6*) **according to the Scriptures,** (*I Cor. 15:4*) **and ascended into heaven,** (*Acts 1:9, Luke 24:51*) **and sits at the right hand of the Father,** (*Heb. 1:3*) **and shall come again** (*Matt. 16:27; Heb. 9:28*) **with glory to judge the living and the dead,** (*II Cor. 5:10*) **Whose kingdom shall have no end.** (*Isa. 9:6, Rev. 22:5, Dan. 7*) **And in the Holy Spirit, the Lord, the Giver of Life,** (*Gen. 1:2, Rom. 8:2, Joel 2:28, Gen. 2:7, Ps. 34:6*) **Who proceeds from the Father,** (*John 15:26*) **Who with the Father and the Son together is worshiped and glorified,** (*John 16:14, 15*) **Who spake by the Prophets.** (*Heb. 1:1, Num. 11:29, I Sam. 16:13*) **In One, Holy, Catholic, and Apostolic Church;** (*Eph. 4:4, Matt. 16:18*) **I acknowledge one baptism for the remission of sins;** (*Matt. 28:19, Eph. 4:5*) **I look for the resurrection of the dead** (*I Cor. 15:52, Ez. 37*) **and the life of the world to come.** (*Col. 3:4,2, I and II Thes. 1:10, Rev. 21,22*) **Amen.**

Then 5 or 10 prostrations (or bows if we are not able) saying/ using the Jesus Prayer,

Lord Jesus Christ, Son of God, have mercy on me.

We pray either for ourselves, our loved ones, or those with whom we are at enmity. We cross ourselves each time and say the prayer as we bow to the ground with our forehead quickly touching the floor.

Then, for at least 5 or 10 minutes, we audibly but quietly say the Jesus Prayer, either standing or kneeling (but preferably not sitting).[2]

Then we say prayers from the Prayer Book/Prayers for Communion/Prayers of Intercession for others/etc.

Then we read a chapter from the Gospels and from a small portion of Orthodox spiritual reading.[3]

Then, if desired, this morning prayer: I thank Thee, O Lord, that Thou hast again shown me the Light of a new day. Grant me to greet this day in peace. At all times, help me to rely upon Thy holy will. In every hour of this day, help me, teach me, and reveal Thy will to me. Bless, help, and save all those who surround me. Teach me to treat everything that comes to me throughout this day with peace of soul and with firm conviction that Thy will governs all things. In all my deeds and words, sanctify, bless, and correct my thoughts and feelings. In unforeseen events, let me not forget that everything is sent by Thee. Teach me to act firmly and wisely without embittering or embarrassing others. O Lord, give me strength to bear the

---

[2] Tempo can vary: if we are distracted, then we pray quickly; if we are relaxed, slowly.

The Jesus Prayer is not a mantra or vain repetition. The words are a profoundly meaningful confession by which we begin our dialogue with God in fulfillment of the Lord's words: "Whatever you ask in my Name, that I will do" (John 14:13).

[3] We need to read the words of our Lord every day, at least one chapter. A consecutive reading of Matthew, Mark, Luke, and John throughout the year greatly aids us in understanding and doing God's will.

fatigue of the coming day with all it shall bring. Direct my will, teach me to pray, and Thyself, come, grant me Thy blessing, be with me, and pray within me. Amen.

Or this evening prayer: O Eternal God and King of all creation, Who hast kept me safe to attain to this hour, forgive me all wherein I have sinned today in deed, word, and thought. Cleanse, O Lord, my transgressions and faults and make me a Temple for the Holy Spirit. Vanquish the enemies, both bodily and bodiless that fight against me, and keep and deliver me from the vain thoughts and evil desires which tempt me. Receive my prayers in Thy great mercy. Shine into my heart the Light of the Holy Spirit. Grant me to live according to Thy commandments. Teach me to do Thy will for Thou art my God. O Lord, I thank Thee for all the things that Thou hast brought me this day and I commend it all into Thy hands, trusting that through Thy mercy all things will turn out for the good and my salvation. Grant me also, as I go to sleep, rest for my body and soul, and preserve me from the passions of the flesh and the influences of dark and evil spirits. Amen.

Then: It is truly meet to bless thee, O Theotokos, ever-blessed and most pure and the Mother of our God. More honorable than the Cherubim and more glorious beyond compare than the Seraphim; without corruption thou gavest birth to God the Word: True Theotokos, we magnify thee!

Glory to the Father, and to the Son, and to the Holy Spirit, now and ever, and unto ages of ages. Amen.

Lord, have mercy. (*thrice*)

Through the prayers of our holy Fathers, O Lord Jesus Christ our God, have mercy upon us and save us. Amen.

Through the prayers of Thy most pure Mother, my holy Guardian Angel, my patron saint N. and of all Thy saints, have mercy on us and upon Thy world.

O Lord, into Thy hands I commit my spirit. Amen.

THE MONASTERY OF ST. TIKHON OF ZADONSK

Located in South Canaan, Pennsylvania in the rolling hills of the Pocono Mountains, our monastery of St. Tikhon of Zadonsk was founded by St. Tikhon, Patriarch of Moscow, in 1905. It is America's oldest Orthodox monastery. Since its founding, six canonized saints have walked, taught, and lived here. We serve the Divine Liturgy, along with a full cycle of services, every day. Our monastery is open daily to the general  public; we offer hospitality to visitors from around the world. In addition, the monastery has one of the largest museums of Orthodox history and iconography in America. Our monastery provides teachers at St. Tikhon's Orthodox Theological Seminary (est. 1938); we publish through St. Tikhon's Monastery Press; and operate St. Tikhon's Bookstore (www.stspress. com). For more information about St. Tikhon's Monastery, please visit us online at sttikhonsmonastery.org or call us at 570-937-4390. We look forward to your visit.